Making sense of capacity development

Experiences with Technical Assistance and Capacity Development in the HIV response

Making sense of capacity development

Experiences with Technical Assistance and Capacity Development in the HIV response

Authors: Gustav Liliequist, Jeff Tshabalala, Greg Munro, Soe Naing, Daniel Kubuafor, Gilvam Silva, Manuel Mancheno, Simon Muchiru, Noemy Leis, Octavery Kamil, Allen Nankunda, Zhai Wen, Siddhi Mankad, Yvonne Ouattara, Erastus Njeru and Boaz Cheluget

Editors: Judith King, Greg Munro, Emily Oro, Dian Zaman, Françoise Jenniskens, Pam Baatsen and Gerard Baltissen

Table of contents

Acknowledgements	7
Foreword	9
Abbreviations	11
Chapter 1: Introduction	17
Chapter 2: Experiences in Capacity Development	21
2.1 The Laços Sul-Sul Initiative: Strengthening National Responses to AIDS through South-South Cooperation - Gustav Liliequist	25
2.2 Strengthening Country Coordination Mechanisms - Lived Experience from Six Countries in Eastern and Southern Africa - Jeff Tshabalala	35
2.3 Fitting the Bill: Aligning Capacity Development Initiatives with Global Fund Grant Weaknesses - Greg Munro	45
2.4 Capacity Development of Consultants: Are we reaping what we sow? - Soe Naing	53
2.5 How Strategic is your Strategy? Developing an evidence-informed national AIDS response - Daniel Kubuafor	63
2.6 Harmonization of Public Policies around HIV Prevention in Schools - Gilvam Silva, Manuel Mancheno	68
2.7 Taking "Emergency" Seriously: Shifts in HIV Planning in Swaziland - Simon Muchiru	75
2.8 Twinning Consultancy: A Strategic Capacity Development Process, a personal account of a local consultant - Noemi Leis	85
2.9 Building Home-grown Champions of Harm Reduction in Indonesia - Octavery Kamil	95
2.10 Flexibility in Managing a Culturally Challenging Situation, Sharing a Personal Experience in Dealing with Language Barriers - Allen Nankunda	103
2.11 Even a long journey starts with a small step, Reflections on technical support in including Community System Strengthening in China's Global Fund HIV Plan - Zhai Wen	111

Chapter 3: Experiences in Technical Assistance   123
3.1   In Unison: Good Practices in TA Management - Siddhi Mankad   125
3.2   Responding to the HIV Epidemic in West and Central Africa: Managing Technical Assistance - Yvonne Ouattara   136
3.3   Mission Impossible - Delivering Quality Output in a Short Time - Erastus Njeru and Boaz Cheluget   145

Chapter 4: Cross-cutting Lessons from the Case Studies   155

Acknowledgements

In early 2008, UNAIDS contracted the Royal Tropical Institute Amsterdam to provide backstopping support to the UNAIDS Technical Support Facilities (TSF) and the International Centre for Technical cooperation (ICTC). In a participatory process, it was decided that this backstopping support should focus on assisting the TSFs/ICTC with, among other services, documenting their contributions to capacity building and technical assistance. This decision was based on the collective realization that not much documentation existed in these two areas. In an effort to fill this gap, the Royal Tropical Institute, in consultation with the Technical Support Facilities, IIRR and UNAIDS, organized a write shop in Malaysia in May 2009. This book is the result of that write shop which had two major objectives:
1) to build the capacity of the TSFs/ICTC to organize similar write shops in their respective regions and 2) to document technical assistance and capacity building experiences of the TSFs/ICTC.

We would like to acknowledge the following organizations and people for their support provided to this book:

- TSF Southern Africa, TSF Eastern Africa, TSF West and Central Africa, TSF Southeast Asia and the Pacific and ICTC in Brazil for their active collaboration and participation throughout the write shop process. This participation ranged from input for the agenda setting to the selection of write shop participants and editors, to writing case-studies and other contributions for this book. Furthermore, we would in particular like to thank TSF Southeast Asia for hosting the write shop.
- IIRR for co-facilitating the write shop and for making critical inputs available for the development of guidelines for write shops, which were also developed alongside this book.
- The TSF Capacity Development Managers and consultants who have taken time to submit draft outlines for the case studies prior to the workshop and worked until late at night during the workshop.

- Our co-English editors who provided critical input for the book either during or following the workshop: Emily Oro, Judith King, Dian Zaman and Greg Munro.
- And of course, the UNAIDS Technical Support Division for their vision and support throughout this backstopping project and in particular, for the support provided for this write shop and book.

Without all of your efforts, this book would not have come into being.

Gerard Baltissen, Francoise Jenniskens and Pam Baatsen,
Royal Tropical Institute Amsterdam

Foreword

The provision of quality assured technical support is central to the effective programming and implementation of HIV national responses. It was with this in mind that, the Joint United Nations Programme on HIV/AIDS established Technical Support Facilities (TSF's) in 2005, initially in the Southern Africa, West & Central Africa, Eastern Africa and South East Asia and the Pacific regions. UNAIDS, in collaboration with other partners, also supported the International Centre for Technical Cooperation on AIDS in Brazil, which provides technical support to Latin American and Lusaphone countries. The TSFs were established following an open tender procedure and have been managed by existing national/regional organisations or institutions on a contractual basis.

The TSFs have collaborated with country and regional partners in the provision of high quality technical assistance required for the strategic planning, implementation, monitoring and evaluation of efforts in support of national HIV programmes. The TSFs have emerged as highly successful support entities in the various regions and, by mid 2009, had delivered over 30,000 days of technical support as well as an array of regional professional development activities and trainings. They have improved country partner access to timely quality assured technical assistance, strengthened the capacity of country partners to plan and manage technical assistance effectively, provided key professional development of a pool of regional consultants and ensured increased harmonization and support of country partner owned and managed action plans.

It is important to reflect on some of the successes and learning which are evident from the work of the TSFs during the past five years. This reflection will enable UNAIDS and its co-sponsors to further shape the strategic direction and activities of the TSFs during their next operational phase, in order to ensure ongoing relevance and add value to technical support, as well as enhancing overall HIV programme efficacy in the various regions.

This publication is a unique attempt to document learning from experiences by those who have been at the forefront of technical support and capacity development activities by using a write shop approach. The experiences and learning in this book all originate from the five original TSFs, spanning five regions across three continents and serves as a useful resource in the reflection on the successes of the TSF. It will also serve as a tool for the expanded network of more recently established TSFs such as Eastern Europe and South Asia. Finally, the contents of this book, and the role of players depicted in them, demonstrate the high level of expertise and commitment so evident in the HIV programmes being implemented across our regions, countries, cities and villages.

The authors

Abbreviations

AIDS	Acquired Immune Deficiency Syndrome
AMTP	AIDS Medium Term Plan
ART	Anti Retroviral Therapy
ARV	Anti Retro Viral
ASAP	AIDS Strategy and Action Plan
BCHA	Business Coalition on HIV/AIDS
CBNA	Capacity Building and Needs Assessment
CBO	Community-Based Organizations
CBR	Comments Based Results
CCM	Country Coordination Mechanism
CD	Capacity Development
CDC	Communicable Disease Control
CDFU	Communication for Development Foundation Uganda
CRIS	Country Response Information System
CSO	Civil Society Organization
CSS	Community Systems Strengthening
CV	Curriculum Vitae

DTF	Dual-Track Financing
ESA	East and Southern Africa
FHI	Family Health International
GC	Grant Consolidation
GF	Global Fund (to Fight AIDS, Tuberculosis and Malaria)
GONGO	Government Organized NGO
HIV	Human Immunodeficiency Virus
HPS	Health and Prevention in Schools
IBBS	Integrated Biological and Behavioural Survey
ICTC	International Centre for Technical Cooperation on HIV/AIDS
IDU	Injecting Drug Users
IIRR	International Institute of Rural Reconstruction
IPC	Inter Personal Communication
KIT	Royal Tropical Institute
LFA	Local Fund Agent
LSS	Laços Sul-Sul
M&E	Monitoring and Evaluation
MSM	Men who have Sex with Men
MTP	Medium Term Plan
NAC	National AIDS Commission

NAP	National Action Plan
NAS	National AIDS Society
NEP	Needle Exchange Program
NGO	Non-Governmental Organization
NSF	National Strategic Framework
NSP	National Strategic Plan
OGAC	Office of the United States Global AIDS Coordinator
OVC	Orphans and Vulnerable Children
PBFA	Performance-Based Funding Approach
PEPFAR	President's Emergency Plan for AIDS Relief
PLHIV	People Living with HIV
PMTCT	Prevention of Mother to Child Transmission
PNAC	Philippine National AIDS Council
PR	Principal Recipient
QA	Quality Assessment
RAP	Regional Action Plan
RAR	Rapid Assessment and Response
RBM	Results Based Management
RC	Regional consultant
RCC	Rolling Continuation Channel
RST	Regional Support Team

SDA	Service Delivery Area
SEAP	Southeast Asia and the Pacific
SR	Sub-Recipient
SSR	Sub-Sub-Recipient
STI	Sexual Transmitted Infection
STP	Short Term Plan
TA	Technical Assistance
TB	Tuberculosis
ToR	Terms of Reference
ToT	Training of Trainers
TSF	Technical Support Facility
TRP	Technical Review Panel
TWG	Technical Working Group
UN	United Nations
UNAIDS	Joint United Nations Programme on HIV/AIDS
UNFPA	United Nations Population Fund
UNESCO	United Nations Educational, Scientific and Cultural Organization
UNGASS	United Nations General Assembly Special Session on HIV/AIDS
UNICEF	United Nations Children's Fund
UNIFEM	United Nations Development Fund for Women

WCA	West and Central Africa
WHO	World Health Organization

Chapter 1:
Introduction

Background

Against a background of steep growth in funding for HIV and not enough capacity in many countries to use those resources effectively, UNAIDS created the Technical Support Facilities (TSF). TSFs are a mechanism designed to collaborate with country and regional partners, in the provision of high quality technical assistance required for the strategic planning, implementation, monitoring and evaluation of efforts in support of national AIDS programs. During 2005, four TSFs based geographically in Southern Africa, West & Central Africa, Eastern Africa and South East Asia and the Pacific, were established. In addition, the International Centre for Technical Cooperation on HIV/AIDS (ICTC) based in Brazil was set up to provide technical support with a focus on Latin America and Lusaphone countries.

The TSFs were established for a fixed contractual period subsequent to an open and competitive tendering process, and are managed by national and regional organisations or institutions. The selected management entities vary from private sector consulting organizations to government entities (ICTC) to international NGOs.[1]

The specific aims of the TSFs are to:

1. Improve country partner access to timely and quality assured technical assistance in agreed priority areas;
2. Strengthen the capacity of country partners to manage technical assistance effectively;
3. Assist in the professional development of national and regional consultants; and,
4. Encourage a harmonized and collaborative approach to the delivery of technical assistance in support of country partner-owned and partner-led action plans.

---

[1] UNAIDS (2004), "Three Ones" key principles, total 4p. >>http://data.unaids.org/UNAdocs/Three-Ones_KeyPrinciples_en.pdf, accessed 11 April 2010.

Generally the work of the TSFs is delivered in two main streams – Technical Assistance to HIV programs and Capacity Development of regional consultants and country partners.

Objective and methodology of preparing the book

Within the context of "Three Ones" principles, capacity development needs to strengthen the skills of consultants and country partners in planning and managing national HIV responses. Consultants are expected to transfer knowledge and skills to country partners in addition to providing technical assistance. The transfer of knowledge and skills should be sustainable with contextualised technical and process skills, strategies and approaches.

The objectives of this book are:
1 To share case studies of technical capacity development for use by countries, individuals and organizations working in the field of HIV.
2 To highlight innovations and approaches which can be adapted or adopted when planning and implementing capacity development and technical support in HIV for strengthening national capacity.

Many positive outcomes from the TSF work across the world need to be replicated and expanded during the next phase of technical support. Indeed, these lessons are not limited to TSFs and the continuation of their work. In order to initiate the process of documenting these lessons, the Royal Tropical Institute from the Netherlands (KIT) and the International Institute of Rural Reconstruction from the Philippines (IIRR), joined forces with the various TSF Capacity Development Managers and a cross-section of consultants and country partners in Kuala Lumpur, Malaysia, from 11-15 May 2009. A proven participatory write shop methodology (Oro and Baltissen, 2009[2]) utilized successfully in other settings, was employed as a basis for exploring, developing and documenting important case studies, based on some experiences over the past four years in the various regional TSFs.

---

[2] Oro, E and G. Baltissen, 2009. Documenting Best Practices and Lessons Learned. Guidelines for conducting write shops. IIRR/KIT, Kuala Lumpur, May 2009.

Organisation of the book

Apart from the introduction and conclusion, the contents of this book are organised around a number of case studies, grouped into two main chapters. Firstly, in a chapter on capacity development with case studies on the capacity development of regional consultants exploring innovative approaches to improving and expanding the regional skills base across a number of continents, the studies examine capacity development of in-country partners which implement HIV programs, provide new and exciting approaches to ensure a more evidence-informed and adopt strategic approaches to maximizing beneficial outcomes of national and regional HIV programmes. Secondly, in the chapter on Technical Assistance Management, the scene is set for approaches to ensure that the process of providing well planned, efficiently organised and result oriented technical assistance to country programs is achieved.

Format and style of preparing the book

This book epitomizes the vastly divergent landscape within which TSFs work. In an attempt to share this knowledge with the wide audience who may benefit from these lessons, some case studies are captured in a more scientific and academic format, while others are written in a more informal and contemporary manner.

Target audience
Whilst anyone or any organization will benefit from exploring these case studies, it is also anticipated that UNAIDS staff, the various UN agencies and co-sponsors, policy makers, the various funders, in-country program managers, consultants, TSF staff and Country Coordination Mechanisms and those involved in HIV governance and management will benefit from this publication.

Use of the book
Finally, it is the countless individual and family recipients of these HIV programmes who must ultimately benefit from the lessons detailed in this book. Capturing experiences, documenting them, learning from them and replicating them must result in improved HIV program outcomes for the millions of people in our cities, towns and villages who are affected by HIV or at risk of acquiring the virus.

After all, it is for their benefit that we are here.

Chapter 2:
Experiences in Capacity Development

The following eleven case studies from different regions reflect on:
- Challenges experienced and lessons learned by TSFs, consultants and country partners;
- Capacity development of consultants, country partners or both;
- The emerging emphasis on process-based approaches, importance of monitoring and evaluation, result-based management and contextualized, flexible and participatory strategies; and,
- How capacity management is made effective in resource-limited circumstances.

"The Laços Sul-Sul Initiative: Strengthening National Responses to AIDS through South-South Cooperation" (2.1) explores the evolution of the Initiative and considers how its horizontal cooperation approach, which dictates that all parties involved participate as equals in a process aimed at addressing country needs, has been important to its success. The case study highlights a participatory and flexible approach to planning and implementation that integrates building capacity over the long-term. It provides an important example of the potential of horizontal cooperation in addressing country needs and reinforcing the Three Ones principles.

"Strengthening Country Coordination Mechanisms – Lived Experiences from Six Countries in Eastern and Southern Africa" (2.2) demonstrates the value of developing country partner capacity development interventions based on evidence derived from concrete felt needs.

"Fitting the Bill: Aligning Capacity Development Initiatives with Global Fund Grant Weaknesses" (2.3) exhibits a TSF response to tailoring limited capacity development resources given an increasing need for assistance in the face of the rapid growth of regional Global Fund grants. Focused Capacity Development activities to support Global Fund grants were supplemented by TA and direct mentoring.

The TSF-SEAP case study *"Capacity Development of Consultants:*

Are we reaping what we sow?" (2.4) talks about the challenges of measuring the outcome of capacity development activities. It also reflects on the need for a strong monitoring and evaluation system, which captures both quantitative and qualitative indicators.

"How Strategic is your Strategy? Developing an evidence-informed national AIDS response" (2.5) is a case study highlighting the importance of National Strategic HIV Plans that are evidence-informed, well prioritized, costed, and results-focused. It also shares the role of TSF in providing technical support to ensure an effective process of NSP development towards a functional plan.

The case study from Brazil: *"Harmonization of Public Policies around HIV Prevention in Schools"* (2.6) shares experiences from the International Centre for Technical Cooperation (ICTC). It describes how the organization contributes through the transfer of technology, training, development of reference materials and studies, and deployment of local consultants.

"Taking 'Emergency' Seriously: Shifts in HIV Planning in Swaziland" (2.7) discusses result-based management and planning processes, including capacity building of consultants and country partners to interpret evidence for a well informed intervention selection.

The Philippines' case study describes the *"Twinning Consultancy: A strategic capacity development process"* (2.8) through which capacity of junior consultants, with the assistance of senior consultants, is built in a practical manner.

"*Building Home-grown Champions of Harm Reduction*" (2.9) illustrates the process of building capacity through a combination of training and practice. It shares the experience of using an indigenous Leader Outreach Model for building national champions of Harm Reduction in Indonesia.

"Flexibility in Managing a Culturally Challenging Situation" (2.10) reflects on the use of process skills and how to facilitate effective interactions in another context. It highlights experience of a consultant to overcome barriers to communication while developing a training package on Inter-Personal Communication (IPC) and training trainers.

"*Even a Long Journey Starts with a Small Step*" (2.11) elaborates on how advocacy was used to effectively promote community participation in Global Fund for HIV proposal development. It also provides insights on how technical support can lead to results under complex circumstances.

Common to all these case studies is the fact that the changing AIDS epidemics and increasing funding for global response demand that capacities of stakeholders involved in national responses (program managers, technical assistance providers and consultants) are enhanced to enable them perform their core functions effectively, efficiently and sustainably.

2.1 The Laços Sul-Sul Initiative: Strengthening National Responses to AIDS through South-South Cooperation - Gustav Liliequist[3]

Supporting national efforts

The devastating impact of AIDS has led to a number of innovative initiatives for strengthening national responses to AIDS, many of which have the potential of serving as models for other areas within development and public health. Launched in September 2004 by the Government of Brazil in partnership with UNAIDS and UNICEF, the Laços Sul-Sul Initiative (hereafter the LSS Initiative) represents a good example in this regard.

The LSS Initiative was established with a view to support national efforts to achieve universal access to prevention, treatment and care through technical cooperation focused on capacity development and the provision of key commodities, including first-line ARVs from public laboratories in Brazil and rapid tests provided by UNICEF. A true South-South cooperation initiative, the LSS initiative brings together eight Portuguese and Spanish speaking countries: Bolivia, Brazil, Cape Verde, Guinea Bissau, Nicaragua, Paraguay, Sao Tome e Principe, and Timor Leste. In addition, four UN agencies – UNAIDS, UNFPA, UNESCO, and UNICEF – and the International Centre for Technical Cooperation on HIV/AIDS (ICTC) are actively involved in supporting the Initiative.

In view of its progress to date, the present moment may be opportune for sharing some of the progress of the Initiative as it looks to strengthen its efforts at country level. With this in mind, this brief case-study explores the evolution of the Initiative and considers how its horizontal cooperation approach, which dictates that all parties involved participate as equals in a process aimed at addressing country needs, has been important to its success.

The Laços Sul-Sul initiative

Having operated for approximately five years, the Initiative has contributed substantially towards strengthening the national responses to AIDS of its member countries. It has received some recognition for

---

[3] Gustav Liliequist, Technical Adviser, ICTC

its advancements, which include a major effort towards scaling-up care and treatment services. The Initiative was, for instance, one of six South-South initiatives rewarded at the United Nations Global South-South Cooperation Expo at New York in December 2008.

The first steps to create the LSS Initiative were taken by the Brazilian Government in 2002 when it launched its International Cooperation Program (ICP), which aimed to demonstrate the viability of providing treatment and care in resource limited settings, through donations of first-line ARVs produced in Brazil to seven developing countries, together with capacity development focused on treatment and care.

With the intention of further strengthening national efforts for achieving universal access to treatment and care, the Brazilian Government, in partnership with UNAIDS and UNICEF, launched a second phase of the Program in September 2004. Considerably more ambitious that the first, the second phase saw Brazil offering universal access to first-line treatment to six Spanish and Portuguese speaking countries: Bolivia, Cape Verde, Guinea Bissau, Paraguay, Sao Tome and Principe, and Timor Leste.

Shortly following the establishment of the second phase of the ICP, Brazil hosted a planning meeting at which it was agreed that the scope should be expanded to better reflect the needs of the countries. Consequently, the following objectives were agreed to:

1 Ensure universal access to prevention, treatment and care
2 Generate demand for services
3 Create a supportive environment through social mobilization to decrease stigma
4 Mobilize the participation of those who utilize services at different levels of decision-making

Following a year of implementation Brazil hosted a second meeting, with Nicaragua joining as a participating country. The meeting signalled a move from an approach based on Brazil providing technical support to an alliance where all participating countries learn from each other.

In recognition of this decision, the name Laços Sul-Sul was adopted. Roughly translating to "South-South Ties" in Portuguese, the name emphasizes the links of solidarity between the member countries.

Improving technical cooperation and scenarios at country level

After five years of existence, the LSS Initiative can report successful implementation of a number of technical cooperation activities, along with effective provision of key inputs. More importantly, however, its country members have reported that these activities have contributed significantly to improving the scenario at country level.

Arguably the most striking results to date refer to the area of care and treatment, which is hardly surprising considering that this has been a focus area since the beginning. The provision of these inputs to Guinea Bissau, Sao Tome e Principe and Timor Leste has, for instance, had a tremendous impact since neither tests nor ARV treatment was available through the public health system in these countries prior to the advent of the Initiative. From none at all, there are today 11 specialized health clinics in Guinea Bissau that provide approximately 2000 patients with treatment, and the country has planned a progressive scale-up for the coming years, which the Initiative will support, together with the Global Fund and other partners. Although the Initiative cannot assume full responsibility for this positive evolution, the capacity development efforts conducted in clinical management and related areas have played an important role in that they have contributed to create the necessary conditions for permitting scale-up. Furthermore, whilst the Initiative does not provide second-line treatments to its member countries, it has been instrumental in displaying the viability of providing treatment and in assuring the necessary infrastructure for implementing support from other sources.[4]

Improvement in the area of testing and PMTCT for pregnant women

Country members have also seen great improvement in the area of testing and PMTCT for pregnant women:
- Nicaragua: offered prenatal testing in 2 municipalities at the beginning of the Initiative, and currently offers such testing in all of its 153 municipalities.

---

[4] Data presented by country representatives during the V Meeting of the LSS Network, Fortaleza, Brazil, 11-12 March, 2009.

- Sao Tome and Principe close to 90% of pregnant women now have access to HIV testing, with 32 sites now providing PMTCT as compared to 5 in 2005.
- Paraguay the rate of vertical transmission has decreased from 37,5% in 2005 to 3,37% in 2008, with PMTCT coverage having risen from 4% in 2005 to 70% in 2008.
- Cape Verde: 66% of pregnant women took pre-natal HIV tests in 2008, compared to 13% in 2005.
- Bolivia: 5,300 rapid tests were conducted in 2006, compared to 33,300 in 2008.[5]

Working horizontally

Horizontal cooperation is an approach in which the involved parties are seen as equals. As such it departs from the typical relationship based on donors and recipients that still is typical for present day technical support. Rather than presenting countries with a set proposal for acceptance or decline, horizontal cooperation is based on the joint elaboration, monitoring and evaluation of cooperation activities, which guarantees that they are tailored to the specific requirements of country partners. This is not only beneficial for guaranteeing country ownership in general, but is also important for conducting sustainable activities that reinforce the "Three Ones" Principles in particular.

Its horizontal cooperation model has allowed the LSS Initiative to evolve considerably in terms of scope since its establishment in 2004. For instance, a key outcome of the Initiative's third meeting hosted by the Government of Cape Verde in 2007, was a commitment to focus on greater inclusion of civil society in the development and implementation of public policies. Later on that year, during a meeting hosted by the Government of Paraguay, it was decided that the Initiative should expand its scope to encompass four focus areas: prevention with adolescents and youth; PMTCT with a focus on integration with pre-natal care; universal access to treatment and care; and monitoring and evaluation. With a view to scale-up prevention efforts, UNFPA also joined the Initiative at this point.

---

[5] Data presented by country representatives during the V Meeting of the LSS Network, Fortaleza, Brazil, 11-12 March, 2009.

The growth of the Initiative continued at its fifth meeting in 2009. In recognition of specific country demands, three focus areas were added: combating the feminization of the epidemic; epidemiological surveillance, qualification of information and production of knowledge; and community sector strengthening and programs directed towards most vulnerable populations. In recognition of its potential for strengthening the links between the health and education sectors, UNESCO also joined the Initiative during this meeting.

Assumptions for adaptation as a good practice
In principle horizontal cooperation can be applied to any type of cooperation, be it between developing countries or between developed and developing countries. Nonetheless it is often taken to be synonymous with South-South cooperation. This is arguably so because it is a mode of cooperation which came from the South and which lends itself more naturally to South-South cooperation as developing countries find themselves without a history of donor-recipient relations.

The fact that developing countries have a number of commonalities underscores the potential of South-South cooperation. Since developing countries face similar resource limitations, their experiences may be particularly suitable for informing policy and programming in other countries facing a similar condition. Depending on the countries involved, other commonalities such as culture and religion may also be of key importance – perhaps especially with regard to behaviour change communication.

Developing country capacity and providing the means for change
The LSS Initiative has four primary means of intervention: technical cooperation; the provision of 1st Line ARVs from Brazil; the provision of inputs for PMTCT from UNICEF; and the provision of prevention commodities from UNFPA. The great majority of the Initiative's technical cooperation activities are focused on capacity development. That said, a number of important activities have been implemented which fall outside the realm of capacity development, including, for instance, the revision of treatment guidelines and improvement of surveillance systems.

What and why it was done
With regard to capacity development, the Initiative initially implemented activities primarily in the area of care and treatment, preven-

tion for adolescents and youth, and PMTCT, but, in response to country demands, it has progressed over time to address needs in a wide-ranging array of areas, including, for instance, behaviour change communication, and community sector strengthening.

Several of the LSS activities are conducted jointly as this makes for a richer learning experience and gives an opportunity for programming additional cooperation activities between countries. Depending on the area in question, conducting joint activities may also be of cost-benefit.

Benefits of long term engagement

Key to the Initiative is the fact that it is based on a long-term engagement between the country members and the supporting agencies. Although the Initiative's cooperation activities are generally of short duration, they are conducted within the framework of a long-term planning process that stands in stark contrast to the "fly in – fly out" approach that characterizes short-term technical support today. This type of long-term planning, which is central to the Initiative, in effect goes a long way to reconcile the limitations of short-term technical support with the benefits of long-term technical support. The limitations of short-term technical support are becoming increasingly clear at both global and regional levels.

> Although there are situations when such support is both important and suitable, the short-term approach to technical support often does not assure adequate sustainability and ownership. By applying a long-term approach to planning, the LSS Initiative provides a framework that assures that technical support activities form part of a long-term process, even though they remain short-term in duration.

An important event for long-term planning is the Initiative's joint meeting, which is held approximately every twelve months for three days in a member country. The meeting is, in part, an opportunity for evaluating the success of the activities conducted within the ambit of the Initiative as well as the general progress of the country members in addressing their needs. The meeting also serves as a forum for exchanging experiences and developing capacity, with two meetings having focused on specific themes: vertical transmission; and prevention for adolescents and youth. To this end, specific presentations have been made, discussions have been programmed, and materials have been shared. During the last meeting it was agreed that this should be a permanent feature of future meetings.

The key outcome of the meeting, however, is a set of draft country action plans which are developed together with consultants and partner agency representatives. This inclusive process puts National AIDS Authorities in the driving seat and assures that activities are tailored to country needs. The proposals are presented in plenary sessions, thus providing an opportunity for receiving feedback and deciding on joint activities proposed by other country members. This continuous type of evaluation and planning is also important because it allows for flexibility in terms of adapting to needs as country responses progress.

A related feature for guaranteeing continuity over time is the country consultant. Each member country has been assigned an ICTC consultant who works with a country on a long-term basis, with responsibility for overseeing general country progress, providing consultancy within areas of expertise and giving input during planning and implementation.

The Initiative has recently started to expand in terms of means of intervention. Whereas it was initially concerned solely with technical cooperation focused on developing capacity and providing inputs, the Initiative has started to show signs of becoming a platform for countries to develop joint strategies for assuring solutions to addresses their needs.

During the Initiative's last meeting, agreements were made that illustrate this expansion. Cape Verde, Guinea Bissau, and Sao Tome e Principe, had previously brought up the need for implementing viral load technology in their countries, and in response it was decided that a joint operation plan focused on installing viral load technology in one country, but covering all three, will be constructed. It was, furthermore, decided that the Initiative's Secretariat will work towards a joint project for accessing second-line ARVs.

The recent development of the member countries joining together to develop new solutions exemplifies the increasing horizontality of the Initiative. Albeit in a way that emphasized putting partner countries in the driving seat, the Initiative started with a focus on Brazil providing technical support to the other country members. This has changed over time with a recognition that all member countries can learn from each other.

An important mark in this respect was the last meeting when, for the first time, a cooperation activity not involving Brazil but two other member countries was planned.

Although not an end in itself, another important benefit of the Initiative is improved coordination. To date this has primarily taken place between the partner offices based in Brasilia. By convening jointly the partner agencies and the Brazilian Government have improved coordination of their activities, and also established a number of joint activities. This has also contributed to the implementation of inter-sectorial activities - especially with respect to the area of education, where the Initiative has conducted activities aimed at sharing Brazil's Sexual Education and Prevention in Schools Programme.

Continued support
The partner agencies focus their support to the Initiative in their specific areas of expertise.

UNAIDS:
Since 2007, UNAIDS has a specific commitment to the Initiative for Monitoring and Evaluation, which involves both improving the M&E capacity of country partners and assuring strong data for the Initiative itself. Along with Brazil, UNAIDS also contributes through ICTC, which has a general responsibility for managing technical cooperation.

Following its establishment in January 2005, and in virtue of being a joint initiative of UNAIDS and the Brazilian Government, ICTC became responsible for managing the provision of technical support activities. In view of the substantial resources available for the ICTC, this represented a possibility for scaling-up the Initiative's activities.

UNICEF:
The partner has offered substantial technical and financial support since the Initiative took its first steps. Its work involves research to determine disparities in the access to information and services; sup-

port to the development of communication strategies for increasing access and demand for prevention, treatment, and care services; and, capacity development activities geared towards the prevention of HIV in school settings. UNICEF's contribution also encompasses procuring rapid test kits for HIV diagnosis of pregnant women and their families; supporting the transport of ARVs; and supporting the external communication of the Initiative.

UNFPA:
The partner's commitments include working to intensify and scale-up HIV prevention efforts; promoting the participation of youth and adolescents in the formulation and monitoring of policy; promoting sexual and reproductive health, and reproductive rights of women living with HIV; and combating the feminization of the AIDS epidemic. To this end, UNFPA recently made a commitment to provide female and male condoms to some of the member countries. Having joined the Initiative recently, UNESCO will target its efforts on prevention as it relates to education. The inclusion of UNESCO arguably represents an important move for the promotion of inter-sectorial responses as it will likely contribute substantially to the implementation of joint activities involving health and education sectors.

Conclusion
The LSS Initiative constitutes a strong example of the potential of South-South horizontal cooperation for strengthening national responses to AIDS in line with the "Three Ones" principles. Through the implementation of technical cooperation activities focused on capacity development and the provision of key inputs, the Initiative has contributed significantly to improving the situation at country level – particularly with regard to testing, treatment and care (including PMTCT), and prevention for adolescents and youth.

The Initiative's achievements demonstrate the benefits of horizontal cooperation on a South-South basis. By planning cooperation activities in accordance with country needs and with full participation of the respective National AIDS Authorities, the Initiative has managed to address country needs. This is inclusive and participative process maximizes country ownership, helps in assuring sustainability, and reinforces the "Three Ones" Principles. In light of its results, the LSS Initiative indicates that Global Health Initiatives and the provision of technical support generally do not have to conflict with aid effectiveness principles but can serve to reinforce such principles. Another important aspect linked to horizontal cooperation is the Initiative's long-term approach to capacity development which differs substantially from the fly-in fly-out approach that is typical for short-term technical support. Although the Initiative works primarily with short-term activities, the engagement with the member countries is on developing capacity over the long-term through an annual planning process that allows for continuous adaptation in accordance to needs.

The Initiative's basis in horizontal cooperation has also allowed the Initiative to expand considerably since its inception. The fact that the Initiative is a long-term alliance of equals rather than a project with a due-date, has given it the flexibility to grow in accordance with country demands and explore new venues of cooperation, as exemplified by an increase of in terms of thematic focus areas and by providing a platform for developing joint projects.

2.2 Strengthening Country Coordination Mechanisms – Lived Experiences from Six Countries in Eastern and Southern Africa - Jeff Tshabalala[6]

Assimilation of lived experiences drawn from CCM members, presented at a high level meeting in August 2008, has helped the Technical Support Facility responsible for Southern Africa (TSF-SA) to develop evidence-informed technical assistance and capacity development strategies for strengthening this crucial grant-governance structure.

Governance space is crowded

---

[6] Jeff Tshabalala, Director-Health and Development Africa (HDA) Pty Ltd and Technical Support Coordinator-Technical Support Facility-Southern Africa

The Challenge of Managing Global Fund Processes

The Global Fund to Fight AIDS, Tuberculosis and Malaria was established in 2001 to catalyze the funding of programs in the three diseases driven by the performance-based funding approach (PBFA). This approach underpins the Global Fund fiduciary architecture, principles, policies and structures[7], and anchors the relationships between the Global Fund and the grant-receiving countries. A central pillar of the Global Fund architecture at country level is the Country Coordinating Mechanism (CCM). While Global Fund envisaged working within existing CCMs, all countries in the ESA region encountered a capacity vacuum in this regard, and so established mechanisms to deal specifically with Global Fund proposals and grant implementation processes[8]. Achieving optimal compliance with the Global Fund's requirement in this regard remains a challenge to the effectiveness of CCMs.

To ameliorate this capacity deficit, funding was made available by the Office of the Global AIDS Coordinator (OGAC) to UNAIDS, and in mid-2007, the TSFs in the ESA region were mandated to provide technical assistance (TA) and capacity development (CD) tailored for this purpose. The ESA TSFs sought to devise effective strategies in response to CCMs' TA and CD needs, ensuring that interventions were informed by the lived experiences of members of CCMs. These accounts were triangulated with lessons learned about CCMs from 40 case studies conducted between September and October of 2007 in 20 countries[9].

The Practitioners' Lived Experiences: what is the situation?

Governance and oversight of grants from the Global Fund is a relational process at country level. It includes managing existing systems, structures and divergent expectations of stakeholders within and outside the CCM model. Managing these multiple expectations defined the planning and execution of the high level meeting of CCM members for six ESA countries in 2008. The collective lived experiences of these CCM members generated a theme around the challenges of navigating the murky waters of governance at country level.

---

[7] Fiduciary Arrangements for Grant Recipients July 1, 2003
[8] This situation meant that CCMs were not embedded in and aligned to existing country systems, structures and governance institutions. I deal with the effect of this in my doctoral research which seeks to develop governance in health theoretical frameworks.
[9] The Global Fund Implementer Series. 2008. Lessons Learned in the Field Health Financing and Governance- A Report on the Country Coordinating Mechanism Model

It was recognized that the governance space at country level was crowded. While there was compliance with the Global Fund guidelines, principles and processes, there was also failure to manifest the spirit that underpins the CCM as a governance model to influence country systems. This included relationships that anchor the governance systems. CCM members felt that the model was disconnected from mainstream country governance systems because of the over-reliance on compliance to the Global Fund expectations. For example, CCM members were unanimous in concluding from one country's case study that compliance with Global Fund CCM principles was characterized by a "tick- box mentality", which tended to preclude proactive due diligence and erode meaningful engagement with prospective Principal Recipients (PRs).

Limited alignment to existing country governance structures and systems was a challenge underlined at the meeting. This resulted in the misunderstanding of the role of the Global Fund CCM model, so that it was seen as running at cross-purposes with existing country governance structures. This hampered coordination and harmonization with existing programs and institutions. Membership participation and involvement in CCM oversight was hindered by poor knowledge around the programming in the three diseases, resulting in unsustained relationships with existing programs. While some CCMs had GFTAM manuals and guidelines, members have not been oriented on their content. This has undermined synergy and coherence with HIV and other health programmes, threatening their effectiveness and compromising the potential contribution the CCM model could make towards strengthening governance in health.

CCMs' members recognized that they face a number of problems. These included:
- High member turnover
- Dominance by some members and limited understanding of the shortcomings of the program design and implementations, as well as of what can be done to tackle them.
- Systems and procedures that underpin CCM meetings, activities and operations were not aligned to country systems, structures and procedures.
- CCMs having no accountability relationship at country level. The learning generated from CCM level was not shared across programs and existing governance institutions. Consequently, governance in health remained generally weak and strategically incoherent.

Responding to the Challenges
Building technical assistance (TA) and capacity development (CD) strategies that respond to this space is a challenge faced by the technical support facilities (TSFs) in the ESA region. Recognizing this, the TSFs in the ESA region decided to engage CCMs from six countries (two from Eastern Africa and four from Southern Africa), with an objective of mapping the need for CCM TA and CD needs from their lived experiences. The process included deliberate consultations between the GFTAM CCM management team, TSF-Southern Africa and TSF-Eastern Africa in the design of the meeting concept and agenda with the CCMs.

Methodological Approach
A meeting of high level CCM members (chairs, deputy chairs, and civil society and private sector representatives) from six countries in the Eastern and Southern Africa was convened by the Technical Support Facilities for Southern (TSFSA) and Eastern Africa (TSFEA). Intensely participatory methods supported learning from each others' lived experiences based on CCM members' different country contexts. This process included:
- Inputs by members from the same country groups, mixed groups and facilitated discussions;
- Plenary brainstorming sessions to reinforce and further distil shared experiences arising from thematic areas of the case studies;
- Concrete recommendations on the needs and responses to anchor the way forward and guide the identification of TA and CD priorities.

High-level deliberations
The high-level meeting[10], which emphasized the collection of CCM lived experiences, had five interwoven objectives. These were developed and agreed to by the TSFs (EA) and Global Fund CCM Management unit through tele-meetings. The discussions among the CCM members resulted in some achievements. CCM members shared their lived experiences regarding the governance road-map that informed resource mobilization decisions and relationships related to the programs of the three diseases. The experience highlighted that oversight in proposal development requires liaison with program man-

---

[10] TSF-SA. 2008. Workshop Report: High level meeting of CCM members from six countries in the ESA region.

agers to analyze programmatic gaps that informed funding decisions. These experiences were interfaced with relevant case studies on oversight and governance, conflicts of interest, participation and communication.

Through group work and facilitated discussions, members were asked to identify challenges faced by CCMs in these aspects; they examined CCM requirements and experiences from case studies, including challenges related to Global Fund calls for proposals. To map out ideas with regard to TA and CD needs, members were asked to present strategies to strengthen CCMs. Group work was done for each of the identified challenges so as to determine mechanisms and methods which would be beneficial in addressing these challenges. CCM members defined the core characteristics of a well-functioning CCM from their own experiences in decisions that informed proposal development, and the relationships that underpinned those decisions.

Awareness of emerging requirements and key developments to be considered by CCMs were discussed. Inputs on CCM structures, role and minimum requirements were solicited. This included discussions and CCM members' experiences with respect to Rolling Continuation Channel (RCC), Grant Consolidation (GC), Dual-Track Financing (DTF) and requirements related to Global Fund Rounds 8 and 9. The timeliness and relevance of objectives and approaches of the CCM members' lived experiences and accompanying conclusions were reviewed daily by CCM members and facilitators.

What the Case Studies Revealed
Country experiences were shared in plenary and group discussions, based on the perusal of case studies conducted in country and mixed groups. The following summaries are excerpts from the report of this meeting.

1 **Communications among Global Fund Partners in Zambia:** *This case study shows that the local fund agent (LFA) and CCM only communicate during proposal development or during the run-up to grant renewals. The LFA does not share feedback with the CCM on its performance review of the principal recipients (PRs), who themselves received feedback but felt that it was insufficient. The situation improved when the LFA began to provide consistent feedback to the civil society PRs, allowing them to preview their perform-*

ance review report and to discuss it before the LFA submits it to the Global Fund Secretariat. The PR's unhappiness with LFA communication was primarily due to a misunderstanding of LFA responsibilities. Their belief was that the LFA should build capacity and help partners to meet reporting requirements. However, Global Fund guidelines clearly state that LFAs should not provide either capacity building or technical assistance to the PRs.

2 **Partnerships and Leadership, Country Coordinating Mechanisms (CCM), Malawi:** The CCM partnership model has contributed to a redefinition of the relationship between government and civil society in the area of public health. It draws together key stakeholders across the three diseases, namely AIDS, TB and Malaria, successfully mediating competing interests. Effective CCM functioning is understood to hinge upon the ability of a broad membership to act as equal partners within the workings of the CCM and to contribute to leadership. Civil society will therefore require ongoing support to effectively engage at the level of policy and strategy.

3 **Harmonization and Alignment in the Health Sector and Multisectoral Response to AIDS in Mozambique:** Alignment requires that donors base their overall support on partner countries' national development strategies. Global Fund principles for CCMs recommend that wherever possible, CCMs should build on and be linked to existing mechanisms for planning at the national level, and be consistent with national strategic plans. Not only should CCMs aim to harmonize funding objectives in order to be less burdensome in the way they deliver aid, but they should also be harmonized in their composition. CCMs should be broadly representative of all national stakeholders in the fight against the three diseases, including all relevant donors and development partners. CCM alignment and harmonization is dependent on the specific national context and existing conditions and structures. In Mozambique, tight integration within other national health mechanisms, namely the health sector wide approach (SWAP) and common fund for AIDS, has meant that the CCM's functions are de-facto carried out by existing mechanisms. The CCM meets as a separate body only to coordinate the preparation of Global Fund proposals, submit requests for continued funding, to resolve grant related issues and to respond to specific requests from the Global Fund secretariat.

Comments-based Results (CBR)
The voices of the CCM members were loud and clear regarding the relevance of the meeting in shaping evidence around the strengthening of CCMs. Collective learning was echoed as one of the positive outcomes of the meeting. The comments below outline the fulfilment of the meeting's objectives and the members' expectations:

Lesotho
"*The meeting enabled us to meet and learn from colleagues in other countries on how CCMs work and the challenges they face. This was useful in filling out our understanding of what we are doing as CCMs. We hope that this networking opportunity will be provided for further development of our personal and CCM networks*".

Kenya
"*We appreciate the facilitators for professional work done - the past three days were very useful. Although we did not directly address the challenge of how to reduce the number of new infections, this helps us to strengthen institutions that are key to that and highlights the need for key players to stand up and take principal roles in the fight against AIDS. We have done fire-fighting work in the past but planning through this meeting has been an eye-opener. We will leave with a focused program that highlights key challenges identified here. And we request a follow-up program to find out what major steps each country has taken in addressing the reduction of new infections*".

These comments amplify the results of group discussions, country experiences and plenary sessions which allowed participants to recognize the need for the development of communication strategies that foster partnerships with key country institutions, based on strong leadership and alignment to country systems. The participants identified priority needs and practical steps to advance CCM strengthening. These included: intense awareness raising, orientation training, processes of CCM strategy development, role clarification and organizational development, developing key reporting systems and structures, and strategic consultation with other authorities and implementers. Participants rated highly the peer learning, and workshop process and content as a way to support CCM strengthening.

Several CCMs have engaged in follow-up TSF support and all stakeholders have clearer assessments of needs for CCM strengthening interventions. For its part, TSF-SA has responded to country demands for CCM strengthening informed by these results. In this regard, CCM orientation workshops have been conducted in Zimbabwe and Lesotho to ensure that the CCMs moved beyond the compliance mindset or "tick-box" thinking.

Continuity of the development activities

Advancing the Strengthening Process

A five-stage CCM strengthening process is being pilot-tested in Lesotho. The five stages are:

1. CCM orientation or induction: This includes walking through the maze of Global Fund CCM principles and guidelines with CCM members on CCM governance, oversight and conflicts of interest. Aspects of partnership and leadership are addressed at this point to set the stage for harmonization and alignment. An induction manual will be developed for CCM use in Lesotho.

2. Review of existing CCM manuals and guidelines: The compliance mindset mainstreams development of manuals and guidelines without consideration of practice and conduct. The review includes ensuring that the guidelines and manuals reflect CCM guidance and other country-relevant governance practices. Where manuals or guidelines do not exist, TSFs will work with the CCM to develop them.

3. Walk through the manuals and guidelines: After a number of iterative processes with the CCM, a final draft would be reviewed verbatim with all the CCM members to ensure understanding and to agree on the conduct required by individual CCM members.

4. Approval of CCM guidelines and manuals: The manuals and guidelines would be formally presented to the CCM for approval.

5. Assist CCM to establish and develop a CCM Secretariat and oversight committees: Terms of reference for the establishment of a CCM Secretariat would be developed and the Secretariat would be orientated on these terms. Furthermore, the Secretariat would be engaged to develop the terms of reference for the oversight committees and the CCM self-assessment tools.

Strengthened Communications for Capacity Development
The lived experiences of CCM members were helpful in shaping TSF-SA understanding of their capacity development needs. It was clear during the meeting that CCMs have been left to their own devices to make sense of their roles in a crowded space in all the countries represented at the meeting. Clearly, very limited in-country guidance and support has been provided in helping CCMs to develop their governance capacities.

Unaddressed weaknesses in CCM functioning will have increasingly problematic consequences as countries rely more on Global fund financing and have to interface more effectively with other bodies and stakeholders for program coherence and efficiency. Furthermore, CCMs are not harmonized or aligned to existing country governance structures and systems. Inter-CCM workshops, using process oriented, case study-based methods, are an effective way for CCMs to transfer knowledge, examine strategic issues, and agree on priority needs for support.

Competent Agencies built
Evidence-informed TA and CD for CCM strengthening interventions are essential for ensuring that technical responses and actions address the expressed needs related to fulfilling this governance model. Documenting the experiences of CCM members and other key stakeholders is one such approach. TSA-SA has developed the five-stage approach as a strategy for strengthening CCMs which will be pilot-tested with CCM members in one of the countries in the region. It is important that the process enhances the capacity of CCM members, while it endeavors to build a governance framework where CCM model is aligned to systems, structures and capacities of each country. Hosting regular forums, which provide ample opportunities to share learning with CCMs in the ESA region, will fortify this process.

2.3 Fitting the Bill: Aligning Capacity Development Initiatives with Global Fund Grant Weaknesses - Greg Munro[11]

Striking a Match

The six countries in the Eastern Africa region have received extensive Global Fund grants[12], potentially more than US$2-billion. Funding from the Office of the United States Global AIDS Coordinator (OGAC) is used for UNAIDS Technical Support Facilities (TSFs) to support the implementation of the Global Fund grants. Despite this support funding, the growth in the size and complexity of the grants has necessitated the tailoring of capacity development initiatives in line with particular needs and recognized weaknesses.

To address this, the TSF Eastern Africa undertook a desk-top assessment of the regional Global Fund grants to determine their general state of relative strength or weakness, systemic fault-lines and unmet targets in service delivery. This exercise was supplemented with self-assessment workshops with Sub Recipients and Principal Recipients in three countries in the region.

On the basis of these assessments, customized training programs were instituted for the Recipients, followed by direct Technical Assistance, and where necessary, mentoring for identified recipients. This process of assessment, leading to focused responsive capacity development and technical assistance to Global Fund recipients, is recommended for routine application in all regions where the TSF supports Global Fund recipient organizations.

Match-point

Despite potential HIV funding from the Global Fund to the six countries having topped US$2-billion, TSF in Eastern Africa was worried. With 45% of this budget having been awarded in Round 7 of the Fund's grants cycle, almost half of this money was being invested in the HIV programs of two countries alone. Their concern was well-founded: a limited, fixed amount of funding was available to the TSF to support these major grants, and they needed to be proactive in

---

[11] Dr. Greg Munro, Regional Capacity Developm. Manager, TSF Eastern Africa
[12] http://www.theglobalfund.org/programs/country/ (Ethiopia, Eritrea, Kenya, Rwanda, Tanzania, Uganda)

aligning capacity development funding to existing and potential problems in the grants. Two capacity development staff members were asked to consider ways of addressing this issue.

Figure 1: Cumulative potential total of HIV-related Global Fund funding (Rounds 1-7)

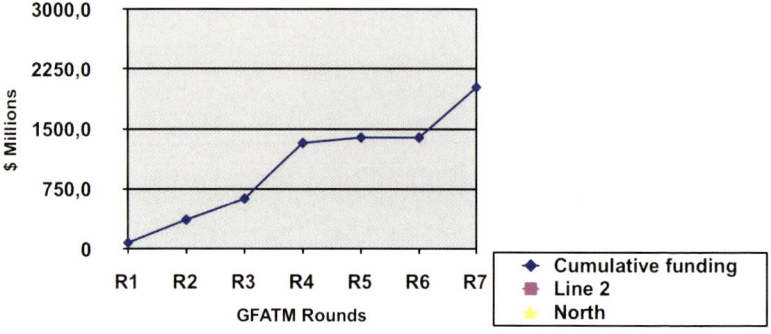

Checking for Chinks

TSF colleagues decided to split their time between two main activities: firstly, to conduct a rapid review of regional Grant Performance Reports and Grant Score Cards on the Global Fund website, and then, to visit three recipient countries which accounted for the lion's share of the allocated funding.

Using a simple spreadsheet and the Global Fund website, one staff member produced a desktop review of existing grants; recording and assessing fund spend levels at the end of Phase I, the overall ratings of the grants and the degrees of achievement in Service Delivery Area (SDA) targets. The staff member also noted any areas of weakness in Principal Recipient profiles.

The other staff member conducted in-country workshops with Sub-recipients and Principal Recipients of the Global Fund, focusing on the Fund's stringent requirements and taking them through a self-assessment exercise to discern shortcomings in compliance. What made this exercise exciting was the large number of new civil society and faith-based organizations which had recently been identified as Sub-Recipients. They were keen to learn, and this was their chance to ensure that they could deliver when the Global Fund money was disbursed to them.

Falling through the Cracks

The desktop review revealed some interesting findings. With the exception of one country, the percentage of grant money actually spent at the end of Phase I increased with each subsequent round within each country – a clear indication of learning by experience. For example, Ethiopia's grant absorption increased from 73% to 95%, while that of Tanzania grew from 63% to 94% over time. The average grant absorption rate for all countries at the end of Phase I was 79%.

Unsurprisingly, grants with a lower Phase I budget (less than $ 30 million) were 16 times more likely to have an above-average grant absorption compared with larger grants, where Phase I budgets were greater than $30 million. It was apparent that the larger the grant during the initial stages, the harder it became to spend the money.

Table 1: Phase I grant absorption by size of budget

	Above average grant absorption (> 79%)	Below average grant absorption (< 79%)
Budget < $ 30 mill.	8 (88.9%)	2 (33.3%)
Budget > $ 30 mill.	1 (11.1%)	4 (66.6%)
Total	9 (100%)	6 (100%)

The ratings of the grants bolstered this finding. Grant performance is rated at certain intervals, with possible ratings of A (exemplary), B1 (adequate), B2 (adjustments required) to C (grant not performing). Fortunately, there were no "C" ratings in the region at the end of Phase I, but grants with smaller Phase I budgets were more likely to achieve higher ratings. In fact, none of the large grants received an "A" rating, and none of the small grants received a "B2" rating.

Figure 2: Ratings of grants compared with size of Phase I budget

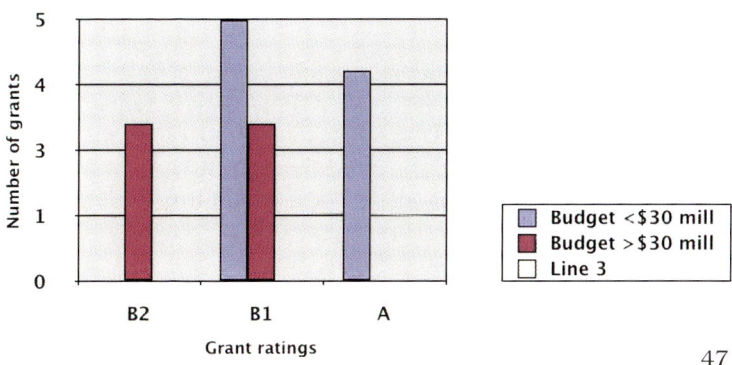

At the time of Phase I renewal, the Global Fund uses these assessments and ratings to decide whether to continue funding unconditionally (a "Go", recommendation), or with conditions (a "Conditional Go" recommendation), or to discontinue funding (a "No Go" recommendation). Of the 15 grants reviewed, just under half (46.7%) received a "Go" Rating, with the remainder being rated with "Conditional Go". Here too, in line with the higher ratings of grants with smaller budgets, grants with Phase I budgets lower than $30 million were much more likely to receive a "Go" rating (77.8% of smaller grants). All of the larger grants received a "Conditional Go".

An important principle of Global Fund functioning is "Performance-Based Funding": disbursements are based on financial and programmatic information. Targets are assessed on a quarterly or bi-annual basis, and the capacity development team at the TSF knew that they had to evaluate Service Delivery Area targets to find out which ones were consistently underperforming. Their completed evaluation revealed that targets were not being achieved in the areas of Post-Exposure Prophylaxis (50%), Procurement (50%), Monitoring and Evaluation (40%), Prevention of Mother-to-Child Transmission (PMTCT) (38%) and TB/HIV collaboration (33%).

Beyond finances and targets, the management weaknesses of the grants also needed scrutiny. Principal Recipients (PRs), being accountable for the management and performance of the grants, are formally evaluated to assess existing and potential weaknesses. In the region at that time, more than half of the PRs were government departments (Ministry of Finance and Ministry of Health) and 26.3% were non-governmental organizations.

Among the grants reviewed, a total of 23 PR weaknesses were cited. Human resource issues - including poor program management capabilities and lack of clearly defined role profiles - constituted 43.4% of all PR weaknesses. M&E and procurement systems each scored 21.8% of the total inadequacy, and insufficient financial and audit capacities made up the remaining 13.0%.

In two-thirds of the larger grants, the Ministry of Finance was the PR. The demands and difficulties associated with managing large multifaceted grants while still undertaking their own complex national duties may need further assessment, particularly in terms of the need for additional human resource capacity to adequately fulfil the role of PR.

"This is brilliant; at last we know where to focus," said the TSF team, reviewing the first draft of the review.

While this desk-top review was being undertaken by one member of the Capacity Development team, the other member was hard at work in the three Recipient countries, conducting a one-day orientation and needs identification meeting with Principal and Sub-Recipients (SR) for Rounds 3, 4 and 7. As she stated later when reporting back to the TSF office, "these organizations are so keen to learn and to get help". This initial contact resulted in a comprehensive participatory process, through which Principal and Sub-Recipients could engage in problem analysis; identify challenges, share experiences and claim ownership of an exercise facilitated by the TSF.

The recipients pinpointed practical and specific needs, the list of which confirmed most of the desk-top review findings on capacity weaknesses. Four main areas of concern were outlined by the participants:
- Understanding Global Fund requirements
- Program management knowledge and capabilities
- Financial requirement understanding and systems
- Monitoring and evaluation

A Match for Life: Turning Assessments into Action
The TSF provided focused support to build their capacity in dealing with the identified shortfalls in Global Fund systems and requirements.

Due to the high demand for capacity strengthening, working from this list, training was planned and implemented, beginning in Tanzania, where civil society organizations have been involved in the AIDS response for almost two decades. In the last few years, many of them have increasingly played a key role in linking communities with national and international resources and frameworks.

The TSF programmed its work in Tanzania to be carried out in two stages – a first round of trainings to be conducted for 13 Sub-Recipients, and a second round of trainings to cater for 14 Sub-Recipients. Finance and Program management training was held for 25 of these SRs and was supplemented by in-country Technical Assistance support for the most vulnerable SRs during the next six months. An M&E training for 23 SRs and the PR was also held at a later stage.

In order to implement these activities, the regional TSF consultants partnered with staff from the HIV/AIDS Alliance to develop training modules and to assist in conducting the training. The HIV/AIDS Alliance also trained a regional TSF consultant in the required skills to conduct the second Program Management workshop.

The TSF-EA team members were able to report some valuable learning experiences for participants and the Facility itself. The workshop dialogue revealed that:
- Most participants had never received training on Global Fund systems and requirements, and that many civil society organizations were operating without formal systems. These disadvantages hampered their ability to conform to Global Fund practices.
- Policies and principles of the Global Fund, including linkages with the relevant Country Coordinating Mechanism (CCM) and Local Fund Agent (LFA) were not always fully understood. After the trainings, Sub-Recipients felt confident that they could be more effective in their interactions with the CCM and LFA, and that this would result in improved performance and acceleration of grant implementation. As one civil society Sub-Recipient concluded: "The whole idea of training SRs and PRs on financial and program management needs to be replicated throughout the region".

In Ethiopia, the success of these capacity development activities resulted in requests from the two Round 7 PRs for similar interventions. Following a similar needs assessment with two Civil Society Organization PRs and 23 SRs, a Monitoring and Evaluation training was conducted.

In Kenya, a PR self-assessment exercise using Global Fund self-assessment tools was also conducted with the Ministry of Finance (PR Round 7) and followed by training on the Global Fund M&E strengthening tool for the PR and the Ministry of Health SR. Consequently, a total of 56 separate SR and PRs were targeted for and received training, 54 of which were non-governmental organizations.

An integral part of this capacity development approach focused on satisfying Global Fund reporting protocols, by offering Global Fund grantees direct mentoring to strengthen M&E and financial systems. This approach, whereby intensive mentoring follows a training activity, will be replicated in future capacity development support initiatives.

Key points for improved performance

1. The considerable growth in Global Fund funding has increased the burden on institutional capabilities of grantees to manage grants with escalating funding levels. Global Fund applicants need to balance the budgetary size of proposals against their ability to manage grants and absorb funds.
2. This challenge also underscores the need to include funding resources for ongoing Technical Assistance in grant proposals. The research found that grants with a slower start-up and incremental increases in budgets are more likely to be successful, and this should influence the activity and funding structure of proposals at the conception stage. Overall, the research showed that capacity development to support grants must be aligned to regular ratings of grants by the Global Fund, and that support for tradition- ally weak areas - such as procurement and M&E - must be supplemented with data on emerging weaknesses, such as Human resource capacity planning.
3. Assessments should be conducted on a regular basis and the results should be shared with country partners. Together with ongoing face-to-face needs assessments, this will assist in directing grantee capacity development work and ultimately, providing an assessment tool for measuring medium-term effectiveness of capacity development support to grantees in the region.
4. Capacity development is not a stand-alone intervention. Resource limits necessitate tailored responses towards fulfilling regional grant requirements through regular grant performance review and self-assessment exercises with PRs and SRs. In addition to training, weak recipients will benefit from direct Technical Assistance and mentoring to ensure that lessons learnt in the capacity development training are converted into practical systems and processes.
5. Finally, thematic areas where grants are consistently weak should be flagged for training of Technical Assistance consultants, who should be regularly updated on these areas. Human resource capabilities and organizational development initiatives must be added to the classic consultant training topics (such as Finance and M&E) so that they can offer a broader range of needs-driven, quality assured technical support.

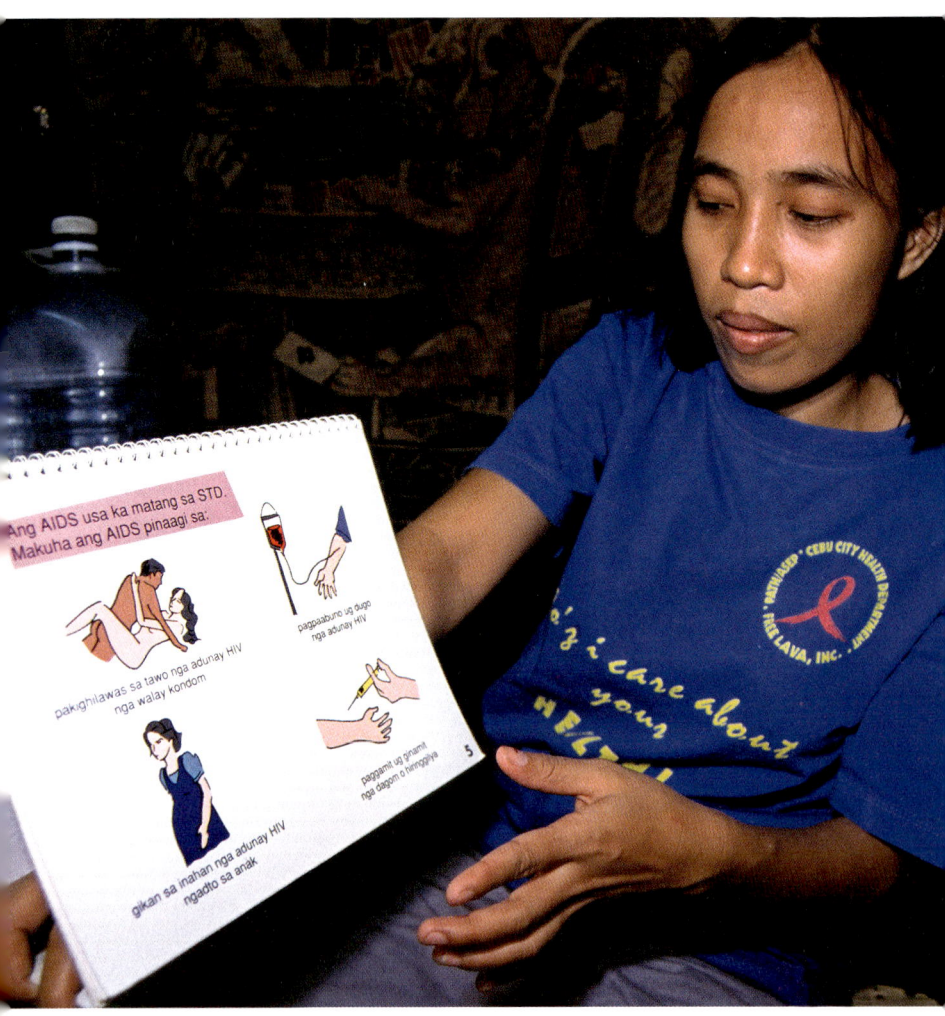

2.4 Capacity Development of Consultants: Are we reaping what we sow? - Soe Naing[13]

"Capacity building is a risky, murky, messy business, with unpredictable and unquantifiable outcomes, uncertain methodologies, contested objectives, many unintended consequences, little credit to its champions and long time lags."
Peter Morgan, 1998.

Technical Support Facility – South East Asia and the Pacific (TSF-SEAP) was established by UNAIDS to provide timely, quality-assured technical assistance to AIDS programs in 26 countries in the region. To enable this, TSF conducts capacity development activities for its consultants.

It is quite challenging to plan and deliver capacity development activities for the consultants since the needs are diverse. However, TSF SEAP applied different strategies to build the capacity of consultants in the region in the last three years. A clear mandate and a strong Monitoring and Evaluation (M&E) framework are important to ensure documentation of outcomes. In terms of evaluation, it was found that measuring the impact of capacity development activities is equally or even more difficult. Quantitative data are do not accurately express the effectiveness of the activities. Although it is not easy to obtain information from consultants who are always busy, it is recommended that regular contact be maintained with them so that TSF can follow up on their professional development to document the outcomes of the activities.

Are we reaping what we sow?
Funding for AIDS programs has increased dramatically from millions to billions in the last decade. By the end of the 2007, AIDS funding was around $10 billion, which is almost 40 times the $260 million available in 1996. However, many countries failed to grasp the opportunity to make a real difference in their countries using the available funding effectively. Among many different reasons, lack of technical capacity in countries across the world was identified as

---

[13] Soe Naing, Program Manager-Capacity Development TSF, Southeast Asia and the Pacific

one of the most important factors. In response, UNAIDS established Technical Support Facilities in different regions to provide technical assistance required by countries. Technical Support Facility-Southeast Asia and Pacific (TSF-SEAP) was established in 2006 to provide quality technical assistance to 26 countries in Southeast Asia and the Pacific region.

TSF-SEAP, like TSFs in other parts of the world, has a strong mandate to build the capacity of the consultants included in its data-base in order to provide timely, quality-assured technical assistance to the countries in the region. About 400 consultants, with different levels of experience and skills in various areas of expertise, registered with TSF-SEAP. It is challenging to fill the capacity needs of such a broad base of consultants from 26 countries in the region, all of whom have diverse interests and backgrounds. TSF-SEAP used different approaches and strategies to fill the capacity needs in the last three years. Another equally challenging area is to document the outcomes of its capacity development activities after three years of implementation.

What action was taken?

From late 2006, TSF-SEAP started delivering its capacity development activities for consultants. As the needs of consultants vary, TSF-SEAP strategized to build the capacity of consultants in two main categories of skills: generic skills or soft skills, and specific AIDS related technical skills.

To build the *soft skills or generic skills* of consultants, TSF-SEAP delivered five-day workshops on "Managing HIV Consulting Business". The five-day workshop focused on three main areas: (1) consulting as a small business, covering business planning, costing and marketing, (2) process planning and management for excellent results while in country on assignment, and (3) report writing. In addition to this, TSF also organized five-day workshops on "Successful consulting: The Process Perspective" for consultants. It was noticed that sometimes even consultants with excellent technical skills fail to deliver effective outcomes due to inadequate process skills. At times, they do not pay enough attention to process. The workshop focused on the concept of process thinking, behaviour competencies, and approaches to create buy-in and effective skill transferral during the assignments.

To build the specific *technical skills* of consultants, TSF organized workshops on different technical topics such as M&E, Global Fund Proposal development, Strengthening Country Coordination Mechanisms, and Strengthening Civil Society Participation in Global Fund Grant implementation.

> TSF has provided assistance for consultants to participate in the following training:
>
> - The Asian Epidemic Model and other HIV estimation and projection methods;
> - Achieving Millennium Development Goals: Poverty Reduction, Reproductive Health and the Health Sector;,
> - Rapid Assessment and Response (RAR), an innovative approach for drug users;
> - Workshop on costing national strategic and operational plans;
> - Country Response Information System (CRIS) training workshop.

TSF also allocates a budget, for relevant, high quality technical workshops organized by other reputable training institutes, to equip consultants in other technical areas not covered by TSF.

TSF-SEAP also realizes the importance of providing practical experience for consultants, especially for those setting out in their careers. Since clients tend to select experienced consultants for their assignments, it is challenging for new consultants to be selected, despite having relevant educational backgrounds, knowledge and skills.

Thus, in addition to delivering workshops, TSF-SEAP promotes training and coaching approaches to help junior consultants in gaining practical experience and breaking barriers to selection. Whenever TSF-SEAP receives requests from clients, TSF explores the possibility of providing twinning experience to suitable junior consultant candidates as a part of capacity development activities. The involvement of junior consultants brings added value to the projects, as they are familiar with the culture and politics of their country.

Achieved outcome

TSF-SEAP has made significant attempts to document the outcome of its capacity development program. TSF-SEAP followed up consultants who participated in its capacity development activities. During the last few years, TSF-SEAP provided different opportunities for 155 local and regional consultants. The following table shows the breakdown of the consultants based on their residence.

Consultants who participated in TSF capacity development activities:

Country	Number of consultants
Indonesia	30
Thailand	18
Malaysia	17
Philippines	16
Cambodia	14
China	12
Myanmar	10
Mongolia	6
Vietnam	6
Pacific Islands	5
Laos	2
East Timor	1
Others *	18

*Other countries include neighbouring countries because the new South Asia TSF is still being established, and TSF-SEAP is currently taking care of countries in South Asia.

Among these, 42 consultants (27 %) received at least one consultancy assignment through TSF-SEAP. Not all the consultants secured assignments that directly linked with the knowledge and skills they gained from the TSF capacity development activities. This has to be verified, as it would be inaccurate to claim that all 42 consultants were assigned and achieved results due to their participation in TSF capacity development activities.

Many consultants who participated in TSF capacity development activities have never been contracted through TSF, but have provided effective technical assistance to HIV programs through other channels. Very often, TSF failed to document such contributions. Similarly, some of the consultants who participated in capacity development activities are part-time consultants, and typically, their contribution to their organizations and communities using the skills and knowledge acquired through TSF workshops is not formally recorded. Unless TSF invests additional effort in documenting these outcomes, one may gain the false impression that capacity development efforts for this group have been futile.

The challenges in measuring the value of capacity development are most daunting when investigating the extent to which the acquired skills and experience through TSF capacity development activities contributed to the success of the consultancies. It is difficult to measure the effectiveness and evaluate the outcome of the consultancy itself. Therefore, to attribute the success of an assignment in full, or even in part, to a particular TSF capacity development activity becomes inappropriate and unacceptable.

Consultants expressed that the capacity development activities are very useful for them in marketing, networking and delivering effective outputs. The following are selected quotes from the consultants:

A consultant from Philippines said: "*I was on an assignment and when I arrived back in Philippines, I was told that they selected me to lead the Global Fund proposal development process and write the proposal. I had very limited time for preparation. Only because I got the chance to participate in the Global Fund-CCM strengthening workshop, I was able to lead the whole process and develop the proposal. It would be an impossible task to lead CSOs and deal with the CCM and other key stakeholders if I had not learnt how the Global Fund works, its principles, its expectations from CCM and CSOs.*" Despite this being the consultant's first experience in a Global Fund proposal, the final product was reviewed by peers as a high quality proposal. That assignment led her to other Global Fund related consultancies, and she is now on a mission through TSF to work on another Global Fund proposal in another country.

A new consultant from Malaysia expressed her thoughts: "*The workshop was crucial because at that time, I was thinking, what's next in my life? It provided me knowledge, skills and inspiration to establish my own small consultancy business. TSF assistance for me to participate in the "Analysis to Action" workshop at the East-West Centre was also very useful for my career as a consultant. Currently I am on two major assignments. One is with the Malaysian AIDS Council for Integrated Bio-behaviour Surveillance and the other is to summarize the epidemiological profiles for countries in the region*". Although she is a new consultant, she has undertaken five assignments in a short time, but only one of them was secured through TSF. All of them are crucial for national HIV responses.

A national consultant from Cambodia is thankful to TSF's step by step capacity development activities for him: *"I appreciated TSF efforts for my career development. For the first time, I joined the 'Managing AIDS: Consulting Business Effectively workshop'. Later on, I got a chance to twin with a lead consultant on 'Costing the Ministry of Women's Affairs Strategic Plan'. Because of that experience, I was selected to lead a similar assignment by the Cambodia Community of Women Living with HIV to do a costing exercise of their National Strategic Plan. The approach TSF took for my professional development was excellent. I think it is very important to build the capacity of national consultants from countries like Cambodia by providing continuous support."*

A consultant from one of the key HIV populations in Indonesia shared his thoughts: *"After I returned from the workshop, my life changed. Before, I did not know well how to negotiate with clients on my TORs and fees. I got skills to make sharp recommendations and to market myself as a consultant. Since then, I am very busy with many consultancies although I got only one contract through TSF"*. He also mentioned that it is important to build the capacity of potential individuals from key populations, because on many occasions they deliver well but only receive small per diem payments as volunteers. Although he understands and values the importance of volunteerism, he thinks it is equally important to acknowledge and appreciate the good work of community consultants.

A consultant from Myanmar thought that when she would retire from her job as Director of an international NGO, she would find herself meditating. However, she participated in one TSF workshop and soon she found that she had become a busy consultant instead: *"Although I have not received any assignments from TSF yet, I was always engaged with consultancy assignments through other connections. I thought I was going to have a peaceful retired life but because of the TSF workshop, I was inspired to become a consultant. I established a small consultant network here. Life is still as busy as before but I am glad because we can provide required technical assistance locally. Clients appreciate our services because it meets the standard and is affordable.*

She noted that her only concern is the discrepancy in consultancy rates offered by clients to local versus foreign consultants. She mentioned that local consultants have the skills and experience to provide equally effective technical assistance. Their in-depth knowledge on the HIV epidemic, culture and politics are of priceless additional value to the assignments, yet clients tend to offer lower rates to local consultants.

A consultant from China said: "*I attended two workshops organized by TSF, the Global Fund Proposal Writing and Community System Strengthening in Global Fund. Right after the second one, I was recruited by APN+ through TSF as a national consultant to develop a community system strengthening component contextualized for China. I was also responsible for making a strong proposal so that it will be endorsed and adopted in China's RCC HIV proposal. The workshops were very use- ful for me in this regard to understand the Global Fund structure as well as Community Systems Strengthening as a key initiative, and to carry out the assignment that resulted in a successful output*".

He also mentioned that because of the skills and experience he gained through TSF workshops and the assignment, he is now regarded as a Global Fund specialist consultant in his country and in the region, lifting his profile as a consultant to a higher level.

The following quote from a Filipino consultant reflects not only the usefulness of the workshop but also the busy lives of consultants. "*I want to express my gratitude for considering me to be one of the participants in the recently concluded workshop on Successful Consulting held in KL, Malaysia last April 13-17. It was indeed a fruitful experience! Likewise, I want to inform you that the experience and methodology that was employed in our workshop had been instrumental in the recent workshop I conducted on local AIDS responses in one of our areas in the national capital region. The workshop methodology earned positive feedback from participants and for that I thank you all!*"

He is a part-time consultant, one of several in the TSF data-base. It is also common that registered consultants take up permanent positions and many professionals work as consultants in between their permanent contracts. Although these changes do not constitute a total loss for TSF, they pose more complexities in measuring impact.

What we learned

A strong M&E framework is the key to documentation of outputs, outcomes, and impacts to prove that capacity development activities are useful and effective. Numbers are fundamental indicators needed in monitoring the activities, but these alone cannot capture the whole picture. Focusing too much on quantitative data, such as the number of consultants contracted after the training, can sometimes reflect negative impacts. This results in prioritizing consultants who are likely to be used immediately after the training, thereby neglecting the consultants who really need to build their capacity but are not likely to be contracted immediately after participating in the training workshops.

Effectiveness of the technical assistance provided by the consultants should be a useful indicator to measure the impact of the professional development activities. However, the effectiveness of technical assistance itself is difficult to measure and depends on many factors other than the skills, experience and competencies of consultants.

Consultants always have other mechanisms for building their capacity, so it is important to gather qualitative data through documenting success stories of consultants so as to complement quantitative data; this strengthens accurate assessment of the impact of the capacity development activities.

Moving Forward

Enhancing the capacity of national consultants who are fully or partially ready to undertake assignments is important. Currently, most consultants, notwithstanding their relative inexperience in terms of assignments, are still international experts who are well-versed in the country and regional contexts in which they are based. They have been in the consultancy business for many years and are already well known among clients.

It is important to strengthen the M&E framework to capture all the outputs, outcomes and impact of the capacity development program. Although it is difficult to maintain contact with busy consultants, TSF should persevere with obtaining regular feedback from trained consultants. This documentation will complement quantitative indicators such as numbers of trained and contracted consultants.

Consistent communication with trained consultants will provide information to TSF on how they are using the skills and knowledge they have gained from workshops, even if they decide to take permanent positions and are no longer available to serve as TSF consultants.

Various innovative initiatives can be devised. For example, TSF could add a section in the consultant feedback form to ask how they are able to apply the knowledge and skills they acquired from TSF capacity development activities. TSF could also improve the client feedback form by asking clients to report on the consultants' efficiency and level of technical skills. In the long term, responses from these forms will be useful to assess the benefits of the consultants' professional development.

TSF and donors need to recognize the challenges and constraints of capacity development activities. Since TSF is a small entity covering 26 countries, its contribution to capacity development of consultants in the whole region in a short- time frame will be limited. Defining realistic outcomes will obviate frustration in this regard. Building the skills of consultants, even if they take permanent positions and do not get a chance to work through TSF, should be viewed positively, and as a necessary intervention. As long as they are contributing their experience and skills to AIDS programs in the region or elsewhere, this should be promoted as a meaningful contribution.

2.5 How Strategic is your Strategy? Developing an evidence-informed national AIDS response - Daniel Kubuafor[14]

Getting one's bearings

With increasing funding for HIV and the complex drivers, impacts and effects of its spread, planning strategically for AIDS has never been more important. Strategic planning has been recognized as a tool for effective and efficient national responses. The vision is for countries to have National Strategic AIDS Plans that are based on evidence, well prioritized, costed, and results-focused.

The Technical Support Facilities (TSFs) have been engaged in supporting the development of country strategic plans, which generally span five years. These form the basis for a one- or two-year results-based operational plan. TSF support to countries aims at enabling them to scale up their response to AIDS in line with the principles of:

- One agreed AIDS Action Framework that provides the basis for coordinating the work of all partners.
- One National AIDS Coordinating Authority, with a broad-based multi-sectoral mandate; and
- One agreed country-level Monitoring and Evaluation System.

Many countries have developed national plans through extensive consultation with stakeholders. This has helped to elevate national commitment, foster engagement and promote social openness about AIDS. Nevertheless, they have not been truly strategic as they have not identified and targeted the primary ways by which HIV is transmitted in a given country[15].

Why is this so? Perhaps this arises from the nature of the epidemic and how it is changing within the particular country. Another reason might be the increasing level of financial resources - such as funding from the Global Fund for AIDS, Tuberculosis and Malaria and the President's Emergency Plan For AIDS Relief (PEPFAR) - and how

---

[14] Dr. Daniel Kweku Kubuafor (MSc.V, MPH.), Technical Assistance and Capacity Development Manager
[15] Patrick Mullen. 2005. Review of National HIV and AIDS Strategies for Countries Participating in the World Bank's Africa Multi-Country AIDS Program (MAP), Background Paper for the OED Evaluation of the World Bank's Assistance for HIV and AIDS Control.

these resources are translated into steps towards achieving the goal of Universal Access. Certainly, there is limited capacity to develop results-based strategic plans.

Countries therefore need technical support to review, update or develop new plans. The TSFs have been providing this assistance in collaboration with AIDS Strategy and Action Plan (ASAP)/World Bank since its inception in 2005. Given the challenges faced by countries, it is critically important for the program managers to identify the expected results and how to navigate the journey of implementation.

En Route

The TSFs observed that requests for support in the development of National Strategic Plans are sometimes sent without a review of the previous program implementation. Perhaps this flaw is caused by limited understanding of the Strategic Results Cycle (See fig.1). An important step in the development of a National Strategic Plan (NSP) is the AIDS situation and response analysis

The case of The Gambia is an example. In 2007, The Gambia requested help from the Technical Support for West and Central Africa (TSFWCA) for the development of a new NSP. The Terms of Reference submitted for the NSP development were found to be un- clear and lacked realistic timelines. With a mandate to provide quality technical assistance to countries, the TSF recommended that a review of the previous plan be carried out prior to the development of the new one.

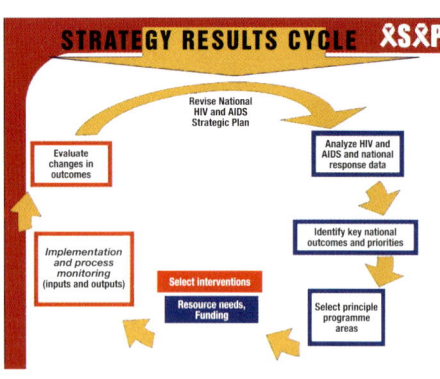

Source: Adapted from R. Rodriguez-Garcia, GHAP, World Bank, 2007

Following a request to ASAP/World Bank for funding support, a series of conference calls was held by ASAP involving key stakeholders (ASAP, UNAIDS/RST, the NAS of Gambia and the TSF-WCA). A critical analysis of the request revealed that:

- The country lacked a clear road map for the NSP development.
- Time-frames were not realistic.
- Also lacking were available epidemiological data on the drivers of the epidemic.
- There were also limited data on the Monitoring and Evaluation system of the country.

So what did the country teams and TSF decided to do?
ASAP, UNAIDS, the TSF-WCA and the country partners considered how to move the process forward, and agreed the following steps:
- Postponement of the idea of the NSP development until additional data was made available.
- A review of the old NSP and the M&E system,
- A research study on key populations at higher risk of HIV in the country to be considered.

The aim was to ensure that the new NSP is properly linked to the recommendations of the situation and response analyses of the country's AIDS programme and the key populations at higher risk of HIV study. As such, the new NSP is evidence-informed and responsive in addressing key gaps in the national response.

Notably, it was observed that the country team desperately wanted the new NSP to be developed before the Round 8 Call for Proposals by the Global Fund. This might explain why the country seemed to be in undue haste to get the new plan in place.

With financial support from ASAP World Bank, the three assignments were carried out with the TWSF-WCA providing international consultants to conduct the reviews[16]. The new NSP has also been developed and is currently being costed, a year after the decision to refine its criteria was taken.

---

[16] AIDS Strategy and Action Plan Program (ASAP). September, 2008. Improving HIV AND AIDS Strategic and Action Planning -- Lessons Learned from Lead Consultants

A License to Learn

The use of a participatory approach in the National Strategic Planning process is a learning ground for country partners. This enhances sharing of knowledge between stakeholders and country partner planning staff.

Proposed roadmaps, work plans, and TORs by country planning staff for National Strategic Plan development may change after inputs are made by other stakeholders, so flexibility on the part of stakeholder is needed.

AIDS programs in countries can be better planned and owned by stakeholder organizations, institutions and interest groups if they work in collaboration, rather than in competition. Extensive stakeholder consultation is required in the process of developing NSP if these institutions are to implement the document guidelines responsibly. An inclusive, participatory and consensus-building approach used by stakeholders during the planning stage had helped the process move on to its current stage.

Allowing the process to proceed without the much-needed data could have led to the development of a strategic plan that was not evidence-informed. Again, this indicated that there was limited capacity in-country to review the ongoing response and the M&E system, and to conduct the key populations at higher risk of HIV study in a carefully phased manner.

Continuity of the achievements

This case study gives clear directions for the principal actors:

To the TSF:
Enhance the TSFs capacity on the process of NSP development to provide backstopping support during their NSP development process.

In collaboration with ASAP/World Bank, facilitate the process of ensuring that country partners are fully ready with the requisite data needed for the NSP process to take off.

Ensure that TORs indicate available data, documents, and human resource requirements (national consultants to be recruited).

To the Country Partners:
Enhance the capacity of National planning teams to prepare and manage their NSP development process.

Ensure that comprehensive epidemiological data are available on AIDS.

Ensure that situation and response analyses are carried out with clear recommendations that can be linked to strategies in the new NSP.

Develop clear TORs and roadmap for the NSP development process.

The engagement of qualified national consultants, where these are required for an assignment, would need to be undertaken ahead of the arrival of international consultants and the actual launch of the assignment.

National stakeholders must be involved at all stages of the process.

2.6 Harmonization of Public Policies around HIV Prevention in Schools - Gilvam Silva[17], Manuel Mancheno[18]

An Example of Successful Cooperation

In 2007, the International Centre for Technical Cooperation on HIV/AIDS (ICTC)[19], in a joint initiative with the United Nations Program on HIV/AIDS (UNAIDS) and the German Government Development Agency (GTZ), decided to develop a cohesive regional project as a strategy to strengthen national responses against the HIV epidemic involving Argentina, Brazil, Chile, Paraguay, Peru and Uruguay. Its objective was to support the countries' implementation of public policies on HIV education in schools that would address discrimination, social exclusion and stigmatization of and among children and adolescents.

---

[17] Gilvam Silva, Program officer of ICTC
[18] Manuel Mancheno, Project manager of GTZ
[19] ICTC is an initiative of the Brazilian Government and the Joint United Nations Program on HIV AND AIDS (UNAIDS). ICTC promotes horizontal technical cooperation with the aim of facilitating and optimizing the use of knowledge, experiences and technical resources and strengthening national responses to the HIV AND AIDS epidemic.

A previous evaluation of the situation of HIV prevention in these countries revealed extensive fragmentation of effort in this direction. This inspired the institutions to host a multi-stakeholder meeting in Buenos Aires in March 2007. During these meetings, findings were presented and technical and financial support for establishing a regional project offered. This forum provided representatives from

government, civil society, NGOs and international agencies of the South American region with an unprecedented opportunity to advance the process collectively. Following the meeting, international consultants were hired, one per country, to carry out different activities. These actions resulted in an official pledge by the ministries and organizations involved in the implementation of national projects to organize national multi-sectoral and inter-institutional management committees.

> Harmonization as a methodology is both a tool and an effect of institutional modernization strategies. Such strategies are particularly appropriate in the era of HIV and AIDS in conferring identity to the Project. Efforts to synchronize identity and action in public sector policy, notably in health and education, can enhance efficiency and broaden national capacity to address challenges posed by the pandemic through multi-sectoral interdependence and a communitarian ethos.

The country-specific management committees form part of a harmonization strategy. These committees provide a meeting space for civil society, the State (and within the State, Ministries of Health and Education) and others, for multi-sectoral decision-making to support the development of sustainable projects.

The main purpose of this cooperation is to promote the exchange of successful strategies and to conduct coordinated actions among countries in the region. This aims to address the flaws in their AIDS response, generated by low exchange of expertise and experience, lack of resources, inadequate staffing and limited political participation.

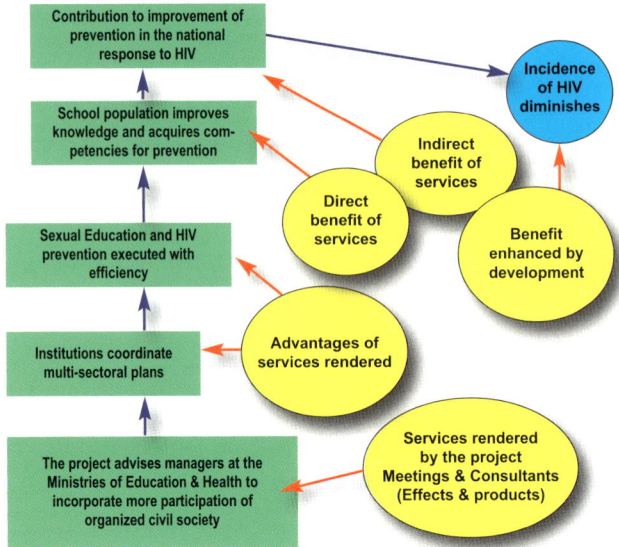

The project was conceptualized from the model of Horizontal Cooperation South-South, a modality that deploys knowledge sharing, referrals for scientific and technological resources, and building links between countries. It is designed to provide technical support and promote reciprocity – rather than imposition – in the process. In the case of South America, these principles are fostered in a context that enjoys great advantages for the development of this model of cooperation, in the sense that the countries share many common aspects. These commonalities may include language, culture, idiosyncrasies, history, social structure and economic issues. This cooperation is implemented through consultants, advisors, exchange meetings, joint planning and training.

Working with Consultants

Each country's technical consultant contributed substantially to the design, planning and execution of this process and continued support in the advancement of the project. It could be said that they are the connection between academic production and public policy. They assist in catalyzing the inter-ministerial coordination and that of civil society, which enables the inter-sectoral cohesion of the countries' National Plans.

These consultants offer superior expertise in their specialist field of technical assistance, and demonstrable skills in communication for management, thus leading the unification of conceptual frameworks, and identifying implementation bottlenecks. The consultants guide the development, reform and alignment of health and education policies. This is done through moderating discussions on harmonization among members of the management committees and providing support in monitoring and evaluation of objectives and criteria for proposed actions.

Strategic Technical Support Activities

The ICTC contribution to the project is represented by the Brazilian program "Health and Prevention in Schools (HPS)", which has accumulated a series of successful experiences in Brazil. In collaboration with the government, over 1000 schools have distributed condoms, promoted teacher training, and developed new methods of life-skills teaching. All these initiatives have offered students, children and adolescents better opportunities to become informed and engaged in the local and national response to STI and AIDS. These also enabled them to discover and disclose their own HIV status, and consequently have made meaningful participation of youth in policy-making possible.

Using this experience, ICTC has contributed by facilitating the sharing of methodologies, training, developing reference materials and studies, and by deploying selected Brazilian consultants accredited to ICTC's Network of Accredited Institutions. Brazil has also benefited from the project through the exchange of experiences with other countries, greater political commitment to the harmonization of public policies, and increased international visibility for Health Prevention in Schools.

The project stresses the importance of financial management monitoring and comprehensive reporting. The focus is on analysis of expenditure and making required adjustments to rationale for outcomes-based spending. Collectively, more than 1.5 million Euros has been invested since the beginning of the project, prioritizing the hiring of consultants, conducting training and producing didactic material.

Evidence of Good Results

A strategic aspect of the constitution of management committees was the formation of the Multi-sector Commission for Sexual Integral Education, which arose from each country's multi-sector management committee, establishing criteria for coordination between and across the six nations. This Commission has identified several elements informing the consolidation of its own structure and functionality. Also, it can facilitate diverse arrangements for refining inter- institutional objectives and role definition of the committee membership to accommodate the various needs and characteristics of the countries.

This level of flexibility and creativity within the Commission reduces threats to the goal of the policy harmonization project. It fosters coordination of actions among sectors and ministries in the different countries, and joint analysis of pockets of resistance to this theme within the school system and wider society.

Led by the technical consultants, national projects have been elaborated in a participative process by institutions and civil society organizations, with the support of agencies of multilateral cooperation like UNESCO, UNICEF and UNFPA. Specific conditions related to public policies and sexual education at schools were studied to inform planning for these projects. The first-phase activities prioritized promoting receptive conditions for rolling out interventions in schools through inter-sectoral support.

Positive outcomes on education and health in the five countries are visible in relation to the presence of the harmonization project. The discourse within the Ministries of Health and Education has shifted and broadened beyond the school environment. The term "co-responsibility" has been adopted instead of "conditionality". This change is a strong indicator that governments are acknowledging their responsibility for guaranteeing effective delivery of education and health services.

Facing New Challenges

In 2009, the participating countries would receive limited resources from the project's joint funders, and the respective leaders would need to determine their respective capacity for financial and operational sustainability of their improved local plans.

The most important goal is to guarantee continued HIV prevention programs in schools without international monetary incentives. The project's success is not enough to ensure its sustainability.

As a first step, alternative resources and new partners must be sought. Ironically, the high visibility of the project may compromise the continuity of the programs in the event of regime change, so securing its future through institutionalization is crucial.

A Recipe for Success
The project has strengthened and harmonized a regional response to HIV prevention in schools across the region. Horizontal cooperation between different sectors in the countries has resulted in Education and Health ministries adopting a multi-layered, inclusive perspective towards this work. New dialogues within each sector, between sectors and cooperation between government, agencies and civil society have been inspired and solidified. Critical success factors were:

- cooperation with a focus on process and impact
- work with national consultants
- use of a multi-sectoral approach

A direct benefit foreseen for school communities is the improvement of knowledge and skills for HIV prevention. This is believed to generate an enhanced national response which would finally result in reduced incidence of HIV. This experience shows that horizontal, multi-sectoral and in-country cooperation, as well as inter-agency collaboration, are essential mechanisms that enable the harmonization of policies and programs, and fortify the regional response to AIDS.

2.7 Taking "Emergency" Seriously: Shifts in AIDS Planning in Swaziland – Simon Muchiru[20]

From Rhetoric to Emergency Mode

With HIV prevalence and incidence rates among the highest in the world and escalating, it is not surprising that Swaziland has declared its epidemic a national disaster that demands an emergency response. Despite this, the response planning does not convey a sense of urgency, perhaps because the epidemic has overwhelmed Swaziland's capacity to respond effectively.

To address these challenges, Swaziland has reviewed its planning framework not only to ensure the "emergency response" but equally to focus on results. Swaziland has adopted an evidence-informed and results-based management approach that incorporates gender and human rights in support of a multi-layered response.

Like many AIDS-affected countries in Southern Africa, Swaziland has developed its third-generation strategic plan with technical assistance from development partners. The partners provided support in the form of national and international consultants who have worked with stakeholders on the National Strategic Framework (NSF) using the Results-Based Management (RBM) and gender and human rights planning frameworks. As conduits for innovation, Technical Assistance consultants play a crucial role in shifting planning paradigms, hence the need for a high calibre of professionalism, creativity and a results-driven strategic framework.

Swaziland's AIDS Epidemic in Context

By 2007, Swaziland's prevalence rates had reached the unprecedented level of 26% among people aged 15-49 years, despite universal awareness of AIDS. In 2008, the incidence rates were estimated at 3% compared to 2% in other countries in the region. With comprehensive knowledge remaining at 52% for both men and women, it is estimated that three out of every 100 Swazi citizens will become infected with HIV every year[21]; that is, 44 people will be infected every day.

---

[20] Dr. Simon Muchiru, Director – Oakwood and Associates Consultants
[21] Swaziland Demographic and Health Survey, 2007, The Government of Swaziland

Just over half of those in need of antiretroviral therapy (ART) are receiving treatment, 7% of whom are children. Prevention of Mother-to-Child Transmission (PMTCT) of HIV coverage has increased significantly, from 36% in 2005 to 64% in 2008. Blood supplies are 100% safe, but stocks can only fulfil 75% of demand. In an effort to address TB/HIV co-infection, 60% of all registered tuberculosis (TB) cases have been tested for HIV; the TB treatment rate remains low at 42% (2007). By 2007, only 16% of the population knew their HIV status. The majority of orphans and vulnerable children are attending school and 31% of orphans and vulnerable children (OVC) households receive external assistance.

The impacts of AIDS are being felt across all sectors of society. Recent studies[22],[23] indicate that Swaziland's epidemic is reversing the socio-economic gains made since its independence and continues to kill its most productive population. Poverty levels deepen as communities are robbed of breadwinners, leaders, and the expertise needed to sustain livelihoods. The nation's capacity to absorb and utilize resources for socio-economic development is severely compromised. Since Swaziland's first case of HIV was diagnosed in 1986, the national response has gone through five planning cycles, beginning with the Short Term Plan (STP), followed by the Medium Term Plans (MTP) I and II, and the first and second National Multi-Sectoral AIDS Strategic Plans (NSP). Each successive plan has attempted to scale up promising interventions. While some progress has been made in ensuring access and utilization of AIDS services, growing numbers of new infections compromise accrued benefits in treatment, care and support, and impact mitigation.

Against this disturbing reality of a slow-burning emergency, Swaziland's national planning and service delivery has come under scrutiny. Reviews of the NSP I (2000-2005) and NSP II (2006-2009) found that the operations were proceeding unchecked, and that the planning process was too diffused to achieve specific strategic impact and outcome results. Almost 10 years after the declaration of the epidemic as a national disaster, there was no evidence of "crisis mode" in terms of planning and service delivery.

---

[22] Swaziland Demographic and Health Survey, 2007, The Government of Swaziland
[23] Whiteside, Allan et al, 2007: Reviewing Emergencies for Swaziland: - Shifting the Paradigm in a New Era;

A New Era in Planning: Results-Based Management

In 2008, Swaziland conducted a review of its second strategic plan. In spite of human and financial investments, the plan had not yielded the desired results, and the response remained "business as usual". This realization has forced Swaziland to ask the fundamental question of whether or not the strategic plan was tactical enough to guide an emergency response. This led to a shift from the current planning and management paradigms that have traditionally focused on service delivery to an evidence- and results- based approach.

To operationalize the paradigm shift, stakeholders were mobilized and through a participatory process, they reviewed their expectations of the desired results and national intervention priorities. Amazingly, it was unanimous that stakeholders envisaged two results - firstly, a reduction in prevalence and incidence rates, and secondly, improvement in quality of life for people infected and affected by HIV. The stakeholders concluded that the new plan should focus on describable and measurable results, rather than merely continuing to provide services. This led to the adoption and application of the "Results Based Management (RBM)" planning approach, which relies on evidence to inform the selection of effective interventions and mainstreaming of gender and human rights.

What is now needed?

This strategic shift required augmented in-country capacity. These skills were sourced through TSF, UNIFEM, World Bank, WHO and UNAIDS-RST. So, a team of international and national consultants was convened to consolidate expert technical assistance in the development of the National Strategic Framework for AIDS 2009-2014 (NSF), focusing on prevention, treatment, care and support, impact mitigation, and response management. In consultation with stakeholders and technical working groups, this team was responsible for developing the NSF along with its related National Action Plan (NAP) and four Regional Action Plans (RAPs).

International consultants were paired with national counterparts, who were selected on the basis of their expertise in thematic areas. The stakeholders, national and international consultants were oriented and trained in RBM, gender, and human rights approaches to AIDS planning.

What was done?

The process of developing the NSF started with consultants working together with stakeholders in following the RBM step-by-step process to identify the priority interventions, describing the desired results and setting performance targets of the prioritized interventions. With reference to available evidence, and taking cognizance of gender and human rights issues, these interventions were seen as potentially contributing to the stakeholders' expectations of desired outcome results. The result scenarios were described to avoid ambiguity and misinterpretation. The targets were set based on the need to achieve specific results at mid-point and at the end of the NSF. The process of articulating the NSF Results Framework began.

This was challenging, because it was the first time that stakeholders were involved in an RBM planning process and also because linking the results chain was confusing to many people. Initially, it was difficult for them to understand the difference between the change language and traditional planning language, and the new concepts of outcome level results.

The development of the results framework was followed by the articulation of the NSF itself. To ensure a concerted focus on results, interventions were prioritized. Priority One interventions were those that had the greatest potential for preventing the spread of HIV, reducing mortality and morbidity among people living with HIV, and significantly improving the quality of life of vulnerable individuals and households, affected directly or indirectly by AIDS. Priority Two interventions were identified as those that had to be advanced given the benefits accrued.

Both the NAP and RAP are the operational vehicles for the NSF. The accompanying diagram illustrates the process used in developing the NSF and its related operational national and regional action plans.

During the development process, stakeholders reviewed and validated specific documents including the NSF results framework. The process enhanced stakeholder participation and ownership of the products. National and regional validation meetings were held involving representatives from communities, civil society organisations, People living with HIV, the private sector, government, bilateral and multilateral development partners.

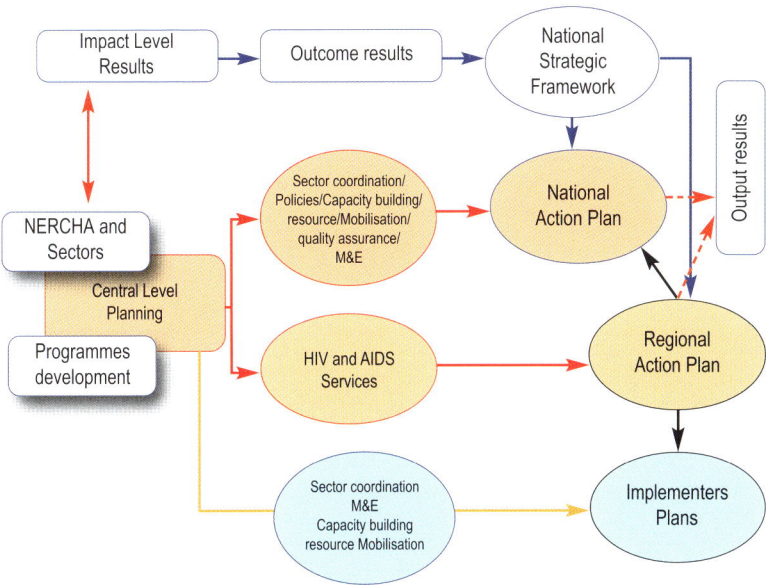

To support the NSF development process, Swaziland formed a Multi-sectoral Steering Committee and Core Team with a mandate to provide policy and administrative guidelines respectively. The committees were supported by four technical thematic working groups, who were responsible for overseeing the technical development of the NSF and the action plans. In terms of day-to-day coordination and facilitation of logistics, Swaziland established a dedicated and effective NSF secretariat.

Outcomes of the Planning Strategy
Apart from the development of the NSF, National Action Plan and the four Regional Action Plans (RAPs), the most significant outcome was the capacity building for national consultants and stakeholders on relevant RBM skills and on the application of gender and human rights planning frameworks for AIDS. The orientation and consultative workshops enabled stakeholders and national consultants to improve their knowledge and understanding of the concepts, particularly with regard to evidence-informed decision-making, setting of priorities and targets, and how to identify and differentiate impact, outcome and output level results.

Learning from Swaziland's Experience
Promising models as well as learning experiences emerged from the development exercise:

Process and Stakeholders' Coordination
The establishment of the NSF secretariat enhanced the effectiveness and efficiency of stakeholders' and consultants' coordination. The secretariat was responsible for organizing all the stakeholders' meetings, facilitated consultant access to relevant information and documentation for review, and organized production and dissemination of draft documents. It also convened meetings of the Technical Working Groups, the NSF Steering Committee and Core Team. This left the practitioners and consultants free to focus their energies and efforts on the technical aspects of the NSF development work.

Stakeholders' participation in the steering committee and during the consultative regional meetings was essential in building consensus and ownership of the NSF and the action plans. More importantly, the consultative process provided the opportunity for partners to start identifying areas of harmonization and alignment with their sector plans. The United Nations (UN) and Business Coalition on HIV/AIDS (BCHA) postponed the finalization of their sector plans until the NSF was finally developed to allow adequate alignment.

Stakeholders Technical Inputs
Stakeholders provided technical inputs by way of participating in the consultative and validation meetings, and having representation in the Technical Working Groups (TWGs). This had two advantages. First, through the interactions, the consultants were able to measure the degree of understanding and appreciation of technical knowledge and comprehension of AIDS among stakeholders necessary for strategic planning. Second, the process created an environment for implementing partners to internalize the concepts of evidence-informed and results-based, gender and human rights planning frameworks and the mainstreaming of HIV in strategic planning.

The Use of the RBM, Gender and Human Rights Planning Frameworks
Most national and international consultants and some stakeholders' representatives were familiar with the concept of gender and human rights in AIDS planning. However, the concept of RBM was new to most of the consultants. Similarly, the majority of the consultants

had not previously used "evidence" in planning, although the talk on evidence-informed planning had prevailed for some time. The training and orientation provided made stakeholders' participation more meaningful and effective. However, during the process, it was evident that the levels of understanding varied from one person to another. Overall, the training enhanced the consultants' and stakeholders' ability to conceptualize and articulate issues in clear "results"- focused language.

Identifying priorities
The process of identifying priorities and target-setting in a multi-sectoral environment was more complex than anticipated for a number of reasons. First, prioritization meant making choices between "wants" and "strategic needs". In particular, stakeholders found this difficult if there was no evidence supporting their particular preferred interventions. Secondly, some of the stakeholders had already developed their strategic plans, and the changing priorities and alignment of their plans with NSF required review of their plans and targets. It was agreed that sectors and other stakeholders would synchronize their plans with the NSF. Finally, in the case of civil society organizations, they also needed to align their plans not only with the NSF but also with their donor plans.

Understanding the Results Chain
Most implementing partners had little understanding of the "results chain" based on the NSF results framework. It was evident that in the previous planning process, targets were set on the basis of individual interventions. For example, the ARV program focused on the need to have as many people on ART as possible. While this approach had merit, the overall evidence-informed and results-based approach was to ensure that resources were linked to priority interventions.

While the evidence-informed and results-based management approach has significant potential in improving the quality, effectiveness and efficiency of the multi-sectoral HIV response, it comes with a host of challenges that reduces its acceptability at country level. First, there is potential conflict between human rights and the evidence-informed, prioritized approach. If the concepts are not well-explained and stakeholders are not sufficiently oriented, the RBM approach is seen as elitist, academic and non-participatory. Secondly, stakeholders were afraid of failing to achieve the evidence-informed targets and hence displayed resistance to change. In spite of these challenges, Swaziland has proved that change is possible.

Continuity
The Swaziland case is unique in two ways. Swaziland had a planning paradigm shift from conventional national strategic plans to National Strategic Frameworks, while at the same time adopted the RBM approach for the first time in its national joint (multi-sectoral) and decentralized planning. Second, Swaziland, in spite of all its challenges, adopted a common impact and outcome level results framework that will facilitate and guide the harmonization and alignment of stakeholder plans, including those of development. The case for Swaziland provided some insights on how meaningful participatory methods contribute to a smooth and effective transition from conventional planning to evidence-informed and results-based management.

Stakeholders' and Consultants' preparedness for assignment
The Swaziland experience highlighted the need for adequate preparation by stakeholders, and by national and international consultants for assignments. It was evident that where stakeholders were well-prepared, the processes were more efficiently and effectively implemented. Where information was available and provided in advance, conceptualization and contextualization processes were much easier and clearer. The majority of the people understood issues mostly from a theoretical perspective rather than in terms of practical operations.

Conclusions
Planning for a response to AIDS in a devastated multi-sectoral environment is complex and challenging. Until such time as stakeholders understand and appreciate the nature and urgency of the AIDS emergency, planning remains cast in the mode of "business as usual". Given the high levels of HIV prevalence and incidence rates, Swaziland had no option but to consider alternative and effective planning frameworks that would yield desired results. The RBM framework, coupled with gender and human rights mainstreaming, provided the option for the third incarnation of the strategic framework.

Swaziland also recognized the need to move away from planning for service delivery to planning for describable and measurable results. In this context, it was not the service that was important but rather the impact and outcome results, derived from the service that mattered in the planning and development of the NSF.

Similarly, the shift from the NSP to NSF framework was necessary to provide meaningful scope for mainstreaming the multi-sectoral and decentralized approach and the operationalization of the "Three Ones" principles. The NSF created not only the logical basis for stakeholders to develop their own strategic plans, but also provided the framework for the first time for regional AIDS planning. An important result is the consensus on national priorities to ensure positive impact and outcome level results of the multi-sectoral decentralized national AIDS response.

In summary, the key ingredients in preparing technical support for AIDS country programs are:
- The use of evidence in AIDS planning should become the norm and not the option.
- AIDS planning should focus on describable results and measurable targets.
- The provision of technical assistance using consultants requires clearly defined terms of reference.
- Consultants must be adequately prepared for assignments. While most consultants are familiar with AIDS issues, knowledge and understanding of local situations is often limited. It is necessary for consultants either to undertake their own research prior to the assignment, or for the client to provide such information in advance. One of the emerging practices is pairing international with national consultants. The challenge has been the selection process of national consultants based on their thematic or technical expertise, and experience in similar assignments.
- The establishment of the NSF secretariat proved to be a good initiative that not only saves time for technical personnel, but also keeps the process moving effectively and efficiently.
- Given the increasing use of RBM, evidence-informed planning, gender and human rights mainstreaming, it is critical that sufficient capacity for both national and international consultants in these areas be developed.
- Adequate time for assignments must be budgeted for, to give consultants and stakeholders sufficient opportunity to produce quality products, reflect on the products before finalization, and ensure full dissemination to stakeholders.

2.8 Twinning Consultancy: A Strategic Capacity Development Process - a personal account of a local consultant - Noemi Leis[24]

Twinning consultancies pave the way to a collective journey of learning. Its strategic approach for capacity development increases the opportunity of countries to establish a pool of experts, responds to brain drain and addresses sustainability issues of human resources. It also breaks the barrier for emerging professionals to work confidently as they hone their skills in the process by gaining technical skills, practical experiences, and greater exposure through short-term assignments.

Choices

When I became involved in the efforts of the Philippines to establish a Monitoring and Evaluation (M&E) system, I found myself logged into an endless learning field. I had not had any formal training on M&E, and most of the time, I found myself silently observing and rather timid during discussions. But my diligence and openness to learn, and being part of a technical working group, helped me to contribute towards the process through which the M&E system of the Philippines evolved.

In 2008, the Philippines saw the need to conduct a mid-term review of its national AIDS plan[25], but national experts were unavailable because of previous commitments. The national AIDS council decided to seek external technical assistance through UNAIDS and the Technical Support Facility (TSF). But the country also realized that it might not always have the resources to commission international consultants and that technical capacity within the Philippines needed to be increased to address long term needs. In the process of seeking assistance, the country requested the inclusion of a capacity building component in the consultant's terms of reference. As such, the external consultant would be teamed up with a local counterpart who would be trained during the process. This led to the conceptualization of the "Twinning Consultancy."

---

[24] Noemi Bayoncta Leis, Program Coordinator, Health Action Information Network, Philippines
[25] Mid-Term Assessment Report of the Fourth AIDS Medium Term Plan 2005-2010, Republic of the Philippines. 2008.

Although the twinning consultancy provided a learning opportunity for me, the offer also gave rise to some ambivalent feelings on my part, because of possible challenges I might have to face: I had entered late into the process, and was unsure about working with a foreign consultant. However, as an "emergency measure" I agreed to the plan, and was appointed as the local counterpart.

Twinning

My many years of experience with Health Action Information Network, a non-government organization in the Philippines, have helped me gain experience in a wide range of fields. We are an active member of the Philippine National AIDS Council (PNAC) and collaborate with other organizations in the AIDS response. One of my areas of work includes addressing AIDS issues by participating in the development of national AIDS strategic and operational plans, providing technical assistance, capacity development, strategic information and documentation of processes.

Health Action Information Network

Health Action Information Network or HAIN is a non-government organization established in 1985 to serve the research and information needs of Community-Based Health Programs (CBHPs) in the Philippines. It also provides training and education to partners in development on issues that have impact on health such as AIDS, religion, gender and sexuality, and pharmaceuticals.

HAIN believes that health is a development issue with economic, political and cultural dimensions. It believes that health comes with empowering people and communities with access to objective and accurate information on health care to make their own decisions and to organize for their rights. With the help of its vast information network, HAIN seeks to provide information at the local level, where it is needed the most.

HAIN is located at
26 Sampaguita Ave., Mapayapa Village II
Bgy. Holy Spirit 1127, Capitol District
Quezon City, Philippines
Telephone +632-9526409 or 9526312
Fac +632-9526409
www.hain.org, hain@hain.org

PNAC saw the need to review the progress of the implementation of the national AIDS medium-term plan (AMTP[26]) to inform the strategic direction of subsequent plans. However, country experts were not available and many of them were also program implementers. Involving them in the review might have affected the integrity and objectivity of the final output.

The council sought the technical assistance of an external consultant to review the national AIDS program through the TSF, with assistance from UNAIDS country office.

The country also expressed the need to increase its capacity on evaluation and TSF suggested a "twinning consultancy." Twinning consultancy is an approach where a senior lead consultant and a junior consultant are commissioned to work together on an assignment. In the process, the senior consultant has a secondary mission, that is, to transfer skills and knowledge to the junior, in this case national, consultant. This "twinning responsibility" through mentoring and coaching forms an integral part of the lead consultant's TOR.

Learning through Osmosis

In preparation for the assignment, I reviewed documents relevant to both the review process and to capacity development, such as reports, proceedings, terms of reference of the lead consultant, the conceptual framework, tools for key informant interviews and focus group discussions, and the timeframe.

I also met with the lead consultant to clarify roles and expectations, and discussed how best we could work together in collaboration with the local evaluation reference group. The reference group provided technical support to the review. The team was composed of representatives from UNAIDS, the PNAC, World Health Organization and the Department of Health.

My task as the local counterpart was to provide assistance to the lead consultant in the review of the AIDS program and to gain skills while doing so. At times, we would work together, but usually I would be given assignments and work independently. Specifically, my tasks were to conduct research, do data analysis, generate charts, provide

---

[26] Philippine National AIDS Council. 2008. Medium Term Plan 2005-2010.

comments on draft copies, document interviews and processes, and validate data. In addition, I ensured that draft reports were circulated among the evaluation team, and collated comments and forwarded these to the lead consultant. In preparing to share the initial findings, we developed the presentation together. The lead consultant presented to the PNAC, while I took note of the comments.

The capacity development mission continued even after the lead consultant had left the country. The lead consultant and I continued to work together via e-mail on the finalization of the report, more data were validated, more charts were generated, and each time, documents with track changes were sent back and forth.

I learned by delivering outputs rather than having a sit-down discussion on the theoretical concepts of evaluation. I consistently referred to the tools developed by the lead consultant – such as the conceptual framework, inception report, agenda of workshops, timeline and guide questions - to understand the context of the assignment. The whole process was a practical learning experience. It involved revising and appreciating my outputs along the way.

Trips and Slips
I joined in the review of AMTP halfway through the process, two weeks after the first commissioned local consultant withdrew from the assignment due to technical issues. This resulted in some challenges on my part in terms of limited time for face-to-face sessions with the international consultant, and the demands of catching up in the process. In essence, we had two days left to work together. I also missed being involved in some critical processes and activities, such as the development of the conceptual framework and tools, data gathering, field interviews and site visits.

Nonetheless, I had to undertake the remaining work. Much of it entailed data analysis, identifying gaps in the report and finalizing it. I had to do more research by filling and validating data gaps, generating graphs as needed and soliciting inputs from the team. One very useful tool that was developed was the matrix of the targets for the national plan' in relation to achievements (See Annex 1). The table provides a quick glance on the country's progress and how much work needs to be done. The stakeholders found the tool very useful and practical. It was fully utilized, contributing to the devel-

The diagram below illustrates the Twinning Consultancy processes

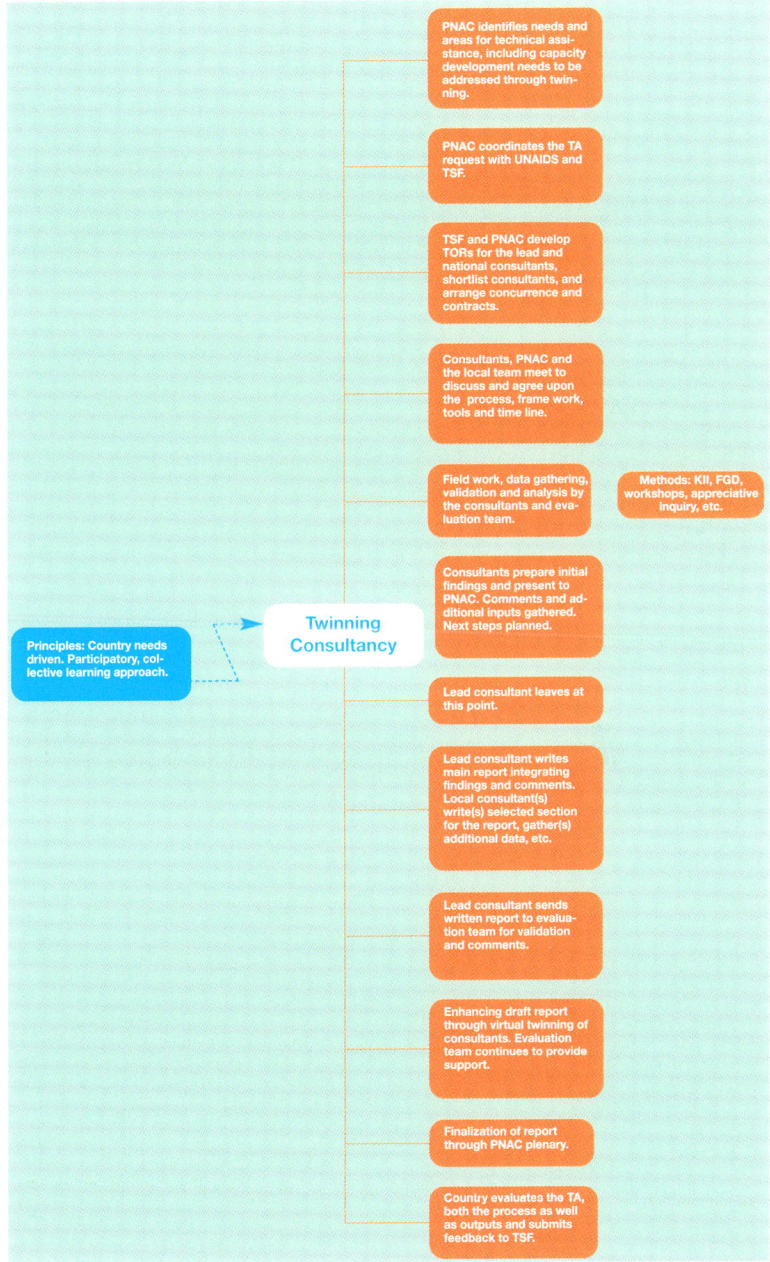

Chapter 2: Experiences in Capacity Development

opment of, inter alia, the AIDS Medium Term Plan operational plan, Global Fund proposal, and UNDP country program on AIDS.

It was gratifying to be part of an output that was appreciated and utilized for critical purposes. Although I had missed some processes, I believe that the skills I gained in evaluation were valuable in addressing the country's capacity needs. My knowledge was enhanced, the experience built my confidence and my self-perception of capacity has changed. It was a robust and exciting engagement, and seeing the immediate results gave me a sense of "winning moments."

While I and my lead consultant were working closely together, the value of having an evaluation reference group cannot be underrated. The technical support given to us by the group provided balance in the approach, in validating assumptions. It inspired me to proceed with the assignment even though I had not had the benefit of being involved in the entire process. Despite the fact that time was limited for mentoring, continuous virtual liaison between us supplemented the time needed for face-to-face meetings. This made my journey to learning through twinning an innovative, relevant, and organized experience.

Building Blocks
The twinning consultancy is very useful. It has great potential as a capacity development intervention and as an alternative learning strategy. The local consultant can serve as a strategic link between the international consultant and local stakeholders because of his/her knowledge on country-specific issues of culture, context and dynamics.

However, to be more effective, twinning can be strengthened by developing a framework that would guide the senior consultant, the country, the evaluation reference group and the local consultant in the process. The framework may define critical areas that need capacity building most urgently, such as evidence-informed planning, articulation of issues, and critical analysis. It should also indicate clear learning objectives and set indicators that can be examined later to measure whether or not the capacity of the local consultant has increased. Identifying learning methodology is also important to understand how it can affect the delivery of the desired outputs. For example, the local consultant may be allowed to conduct actual facilitation of workshops, interviews and focus group discussions.

In the selection of the twinning consultants, attention should be given to their understanding of and their experience with inclusive and participatory planning. Participatory planning is crucial to ensure that the country is informed and various voices are heard, and guarantees that selection criteria are clear and agreed upon by key stakeholders. The principle of inclusion must be observed by the consultants in the process and accountability to stakeholders should be emphasized. Inclusion means ensuring the involvement of all stakeholders and in instances where resources are limited, logical selection of representatives of sites and population should be carefully considered. While accountability refers to the consultants' responsibility not only to deliver output to TSF but also to provide required quality information which can be utilized by the country for planning for the community at large and people living with HIV. After all, they are the ultimate recipients of the efforts.

Continuity

In addition and for long-term benefits, country partners should also find ways to manage and retain the trained local consultants in the pool of experts for their future needs, while still treating them as independent. In some African countries, local consultants are retained in the national pool of experts by maintaining a database, involving the consultants in other country processes and developing guidelines to maximise the expertise of the trained local consultants. They still work independently, but capacity building of the local experts should continue. Although national consultants have received training and have substantial experience, TSF should continue to provide training opportunities and more exposure for consultants to address continuing capacity building of junior consultants in response to needs and changing trends of the epidemic. Learning is an endless process, as is TSF's role in providing capacity development.

Lastly, it is crucial to consider the lead consultant's view on the role of mentor and coach and how well he/she is able to respond to the requirements of the twinning consultancy. Is the lead consultant willing to train a local counterpart? What are the mentoring and coaching skills of the lead consultant? How well is the lead consultant able to transfer knowledge and skills? Is the lead consultant able to define the weaker and stronger sides of the junior consultant and define his/her learning needs? How will the lead consultant be able to measure the capacity that has been built as result of the twinning assignment and could he/she set indicators for this? And lastly, is the senior consultant capable to provide constructive feedback to the junior consultant and define critical areas that need follow-up?

Final Note

The concept of twinning consultancy is a potential alternative capacity development strategy in addressing country and human resources needs. It contributes to the delivery of desired outputs in the appropriate context. At the micro-level, it builds a specialized skill for both the individual and the organization, and increases opportunities for collaboration.

In the context of development work, "twinning, seen as technical assistance with the ultimate goal of producing a critical mass of evaluators (or experts), is an effective and cheap way to attain that goal."[27]

---

[27] Interview with Dr. Jessie Fantone, M&E Officer, PNAC. May 11, 2009.

Annex 1: Sample Matrix of national plan's targets vs. achievements Program Progress

Denominator used in calculating the percentage of targets achieved is based in the denominator provided in column 4.

Sub-population	Universal Access Targets (%)	Amtp4 Targets in percentage and actual number 2008	Denominator in figures (source 2007) Estimates of PLHIV (adults) in the Philippines, [2008])	Targets Achieved (quote source)
MSM	Reached by prevention program: 2008: 30% 2010: 60%	Reached by prevention program: 2008: 30% (200,797) 2010: 60% (401,594) Additional: GFr3: 13,150 GFr5: 4000	669,323	Reached by prevention program: 19% (127,154) UNGASS 2008 Additional: GF3: 2% (14,530) GF5: 0.83% (5,564)
	Knowledge: 2008: 90% 2010: 90%	Knowledge: 2008: 90 (602,391) 2010: 90 (602,391)		Knowledge: 10% (66,932) UNGASS 2008
	Condom use: 2008: 85% 2010: 95%	Condom use: 2008: 85% (568,925) 2010: 95% (635,857)		Condom use: 32% (214,183) UNGASS 2008
		HIV tested and know the results: 2008:15% (100,398) 2010: 30% (200,797)		HIV tested and know the results 16% (107,092) UNGASS 2008
IDU	Reached by prevention program: 2008: 30% 2010: 60%	Reached by prevention program: 2008: 30% (6,095) 2010: 60% (12,197) Additional: GFr5: 500	20,316	14% (2,844) UNGASS 08 Additional: GFr5: 4.4% (899)
	Knowledge: 2008: 90% 2010: 90%	Knowledge: 2008: 90% (18,284) 2010: 90% (18,284)		Knowledge: 26% (5,282) UNGASS 08
	Condom use: 2008: 50% 2010: 85%	Condom use: 2008: 50% (10,158) 2010: 85% (17,267)		No data
	Use of sterile equipment 2008: 50% 2010: 50%	Use of sterile equipment: 2008: 50% (10,158) 2010: 50% (10,158)		Use of sterile eqpt: 48% (9,752) UNGASS 07
		HIV tested and know the the results: 2008: 15% (3,047) 2010: 30% (6,095)		HIV tested and know results: 4% (813) UNGASS 08
		STI prevalence: 2008: 5% (1,016) 2010: 2.5% (508)		No data

2.9 Building Home-grown Champions of Harm Reduction in Indonesia - Octavery Kamil[28]

Husen is a program manager in Yakita Foundation, a Harm Reduction NGO in Bogor, West Java, for the last three years. He was an injecting drug user and has been incarcerated. He became a peer educator, an outreach worker, a field coordinator and finally a project manager on the program. Now he leads 16 staff on an HIV prevention project. He knows what he wants to pursue in his life, and rejects the opinion that it is not worthwhile to work with drug addicts. He broke the myths that "an addict will always be an addict" and that "addicts can't contribute to the society". He is now a young leader on Harm Reduction in Indonesia. His participation in the capacity development programme for local consultants has contributed to his leadership skills.

AIDS in Indonesia

According to UNAIDS and WHO, the HIV epidemic in Indonesia is one of the fastest growing in Asia. The Indonesian Ministry of Health estimated that there were about 200,000 Indonesians living with HIV in 2006. Injecting drug use has been the primary source of HIV infection. Sexual transmission is now accounting for an increasing number of new HIV infections, but many link back to injecting drug use. In 2006, the Ministry of Health also estimated that there were over 200,000 IDU in the country's largest cities. This problem is a recent phenomenon originating from the heroin epidemic in Indonesia in the mid-1990s, which increased considerably from 1996 to 2000. This has been attributed to the social, economic and political crisis after the so-called New Order regime of President Suharto ended in 1998.

In 2003, WHO strongly advocated for a scaled-up AIDS program in Indonesia, including an advanced Harm Reduction Program to reduce HIV infection among injecting drug users.

Responding to this issue, Family Health International (FHI), an international non-government organization (NGO) working on AIDS, scaled up its IDU interventions. By 2005, the program was supporting 24 projects in six provinces. To cope with increasing demands

---

[28] Octavery Kamil, Consultant of IDU Intervention Unit, FHI Indonesia

> **Family Health International** is an International NGO with headquarters based in the USA. FHI has been operating to support and manage an HIV Program in Indonesia since 1995. Part of its strategy is to work in areas with the highest incidence of HIV and populated by most at-risk populations.
>
> Address: ASA Program/ FHI,
> Komplek Departemen Kesehatan RI, Jalan Percetakan
> Negara No. 29, Jakarta Indonesia

and to ensure impact, FHI created a separate IDU unit within its program.

Adapting the "Indigenous Leader Outreach Model"

Using the results from a Rapid Assessment and Response process conducted in year 2000, three projects were developed in Jakarta, the capital city. The intervention projects used the Indigenous Leader Outreach Model, an intervention model developed in Chicago, USA, adapted to Indonesian context. The model is built around outreach. Former injecting drug users are employed as outreach workers to increase the credibility of the program as well as the access to this typically hidden population. Through outreach information, the means to reduce HIV transmission can be provided in the natural setting. When trust has been established between project staff and the IDU in the community, referrals can be made to other services related to health, HIV and other social problems as needed.

The expansion of the program and the creation of an IDU intervention unit at FHI meant that additional staff could be recruited. This resulted in a unit of seven technical staff consisting of a unit chief, two IDU technical officers placed in the FHI country office, and four IDU technical officers placed in provincial offices. Out of the six technical officers, four were former injecting drug users. This raised some issues with a number of people who were cynical or worried that former IDUs would not perform as expected or would suffer from relapse. All IDU officers received orientation training as staff of the IDU intervention unit in the FHI country office. They were also trained in monitoring IDU interventions within their area and how to provide technical assistance to partner NGOs.

Preparing for and facing the "Harm Reduction Battle"

Soon after its establishment, the FHI IDU unit recognized that in order to improve the quality of its interventions, capacity building of human resources was urgently needed. In addition, the unit realized that local capacity on Harm Reduction in general required strengthening. In 2007, the IDU unit designed a human resources training targeting 300 NGO staff from 24 NGO partners. The trainees consisted of staff working in the communities and prisons in six provinces. Taking into account time, human and financial resource limitations, it was decided to conduct the training in three intakes, with each intake receiving three parallel classes.

Simultaneously, the IDU Unit developed a capacity building program for their IDU officers and project staff. The goal was to develop a core group of local experts who could support Harm Reduction efforts in their area of work, by either providing direct support to their own project, or supporting the efforts of others such as local AIDS commissions or the Department of Health at provincial/ district level.

The diagram below shows the key activities involved in the capacity development conducted by the IDU Intervention Unit.

Capacity development process

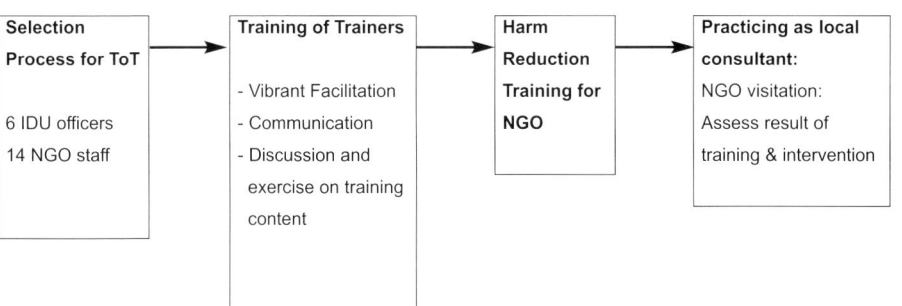

The selection process
The goal was to establish a core team of local experts on Harm Reduction with the skills to provide technical assistance and training. This team was expected to boost the capacity of local players in implementing and developing harm reduction program.

For the selection process for this core team, the FHI IDU unit distributed application forms for a Training of Trainers to NGO partners. The form requested information about the applicant's experience in programming and training, the person's personal understanding of and view on harm reduction, and their career vision. Interested applicants could submit the completed form. The selection of participants was based on a review of the application form data but also on feedback from the provincial officers, who were familiar with and had a sense of performance of the project staff within their working area. From this process, 20 team members were recruited. Six candidates were IDU officers from the program, and the others were recruited from NGO project staff. They consisted of project managers, field coordinators, and outreach/ field workers.

The Training of Trainers
The Training of Trainers (TOT) was designed by the FHI IDU Unit in collaboration with an organization with a solid training reputation and an individual consultant with communication expertise. The core team was invited to participate in the 10-day ToT. Four days of the training were spent on facilitation skills and two on communication skills. The remaining four days were used to discuss and become familiar with the training contents. Towards the end of the training, all participants had to develop a detailed plan on how they would deliver the training. Throughout the training, participants were encouraged to share experiences and skills.

The participants as trainers
After undergoing the ToT, the participants were ready to take on the trainer role. They conducted the Harm Reduction training for 24 NGO partners. This training was conducted in three intakes, each having three parallel classes. Each class had two trainers facilitating each session. Every afternoon, the team of facilitators had short debriefing sessions to discuss and reflect on their experiences from each class. Facilitators shared the challenges they had faced in class and insights gained. Most of training participants were excited by the process. They felt they could facilitate their class well and enjoyed the experience.

The participants as consultants
The next step of the capacity development process was for the core team to follow up on the results of the Harm Reduction training. This

step took six months. Due to budget constraints, only half of the core team was involved in this activity. Six of them were FHI staff, and the other six were from NGOs. A one-day briefing was organized during which the team of "consultants" discussed how they would conduct the assessment and how they would take turns in leading the process. They rehearsed how to conduct the interview and developed appropriate guidelines. IDU officers also shared their experiences in providing technical assistance. They shared tips on being an effective consultant and these were discussed among the team. The briefing also covered specific areas related to technical aspects of program implementation, such as rapid assessments and developing programs in prison. This triggered group discussion on practical issues arising from the field.

Following the one-day briefing, the team of 12 participant consultants were deployed to conduct assessments within different NGOs in various geographical areas. Participants were assigned to take on the "consultant role" to assess their designated NGO. Their main task was to determine how the previous training had been used to support their interventions. The other task was to assess the intervention situation in the local area. This activity included discussion and interviews with NGO staff (field staff, counsellor, and project manager) and local stakeholders (local AIDS commission, and staff of the health department at district level). At the end of the trip, each consultant was required to submit a report based on their findings during the field visit.

A pair of consultants, which consisted of one IDU officer and one NGO staff member, visited two NGOs per week. In each NGO, the consultants stayed for two to three days. On the first day, they listened to a presentation by the NGO followed by discussions with all NGO staff as a group. On the following day, they conducted individual and small group discussions with the outreach team. This method helped them to understand the wider picture and to obtain more detailed information on what was happening within the NGO. The team also spent time in the field and met with the target group, and sometimes with other stakeholders while being accompanied by the NGO staff. During the visit they facilitated discussion to analyze the situation, and together with NGO staff, developed recommendations on how to improve program performance. Not all of the issues raised during the visit were resolved, but for the most part, given the consultants' long and valuable experiences in the same field; they could provide ideas or suggestions for consideration by the NGO. In most cases, their input was perceived to be concrete and valuable by their colleagues and the NGO staff visited.

On their return from the field trip, all consultants submitted a report to the IDU Unit. All of them did very well in their assignment. They provided useful comments and feedback to each visited NGO. Being trusted to conduct an assessment for a peer NGO was acknowledged as a positive and meaningful experience for them.

"Thinking about this capacity development process I had undergone, I know it had great effect on me. It refreshed my knowledge on Harm Reduction. Being a trainer, besides facilitating people to learn new things, it also made me relearn things I had learned before. It also improved my skills that would enable me to participate in HIV prevention efforts among injecting drugs users on a bigger scale" - Rondi, IDU officer, Trainer.

Twenty participants gave positive feedback on the capacity building process they had undergone. Most of them said that the two events (training and field visit assignment) provided them with priceless experiences of acting in a consultant role and providing technical assistance when they visited other NGOs. Both experiences boosted their confidence in providing assistance to other organizations or institutions.

Winning the "Harm Reduction Battle"
How would the participants sustain the skills and confidence they gained through the process? Participants offered interesting perspectives on this issue. Some of them said that after the process they tried to be more proactive in building relations with the local AIDS commission. They offered assistance to the local AIDS commission for training, or facilitating events or assessment processes. Another participant said he offered his expertise and used it to build better relations with correctional institutions in his area.

At the end of phase II of the HIV Intervention program of FHI in Indonesia, the result showed that about 36,000 injecting drugs users in the communities have been served by the 24 NGOs in six provinces. More than 40,000 inmates from 39 correctional facilities have been reached with AIDS program services. For IDU in communities, the services included access to information related to HIV and drugs, risk reduction counselling, needle syringe program, voluntary counselling and testing for HIV, case management, support groups, and referral to other services related to HIV and drug dependent problems. Inmates in correctional facilities, who are mostly drug users (almost half of whom are injecting drug users), have been reached with information related to AIDS and drug dependence and harm reduction. Most of the correctional facilities where NGOs work have peer education programs and have better access to external services related to AIDS and drug dependent services.

The latest Integrated Biological and Behavioural Survey (IBBS) which was conducted by the Department of Health revealed some impacts of the harm reduction program. Needle exchange programs (NEP) have achieved high coverage in some cities, and these cities tend to have lower prevalence of injection equipment sharing among IDUs.

Apart from the positive evidence described some participants also shared some suggestions on how to improve the process:

"I do appreciate the process we had as trainers and on being a consultant visiting other NGOs. It was really meaningful to me. I like the briefing which was held before we went to the field. Sharing experiences with IDU officers gave me more concrete things on what we need to do to provide technical assistance. But I think it will be better if we get it in a more systematic way. Maybe through a session about being a consultant?" (Afi, NGO staff, Trainer).

Not long after the capacity building development process was completed, UNAIDS Indonesia recruited AIDS NGO activists in Java to take a part in a mentoring program to build local consultants in Indonesia. The training included subjects as how the non-profit sector works and how to work as consultant, including how to develop a scope of work, and how to provide technical assistance. This training exactly fulfilled the suggestions made by some core team members after the capacity development process. Members of this core team were also involved in the training provided by UNAIDS.

"Our Training of Trainers and exercise on visiting other NGOs in the role of a consultant gave me practical experience. UNAIDS training

completed it, since it gave me better systematic insight into the role of a consultant. If we can combine both, I think we will have a good method to create strong local consultants ..." (Husen, NGO staff, Trainer).

Based on these results, it could be said that the program implemented by the NGO showed positive outcomes. Currently, from 20 core team members who were involved in the capacity development process, at least 14 of them are ready to be local consultants providing technical assistance on Harm Reduction program development to other areas within Indonesia. This can contribute to better quality in the implementation of the Harm Reduction program in general.

Lessons from the Battle

Reviewing the experience as a whole, there are some lessons that can be derived from the process. To build capacity of local consultants, it is important to provide opportunity to have practical experience alongside training. Local consultants could provide technical assistance that is contextually closer to the reality of the clients. In a situation where technical assistance depends on national consultants not fully equipped for the required tasks, sometimes support cannot be provided as needed. Building local capacity will provide better access and more available resources at the local level.

Feedback from the core team members about shaping the consulting skills in a more systematic way is an important note for capacity development in the future. Although at the end of the process the IDU unit did not fill this gap, it became a valuable lesson for improvement.

This case study serves as a model on capacity development for local resources. The selection process of candidates that considered commitment, good basic understanding of harm reduction programs, being positive and a believer in the program, as well as the building of commitment over time during the process, are important. The participant consultant could be someone with or without a history of injecting drug use. This method of combining training of trainers with applied experience in training and technical assistance consultancy creates a foundation for producing more *Husens* in the field of Harm Reduction.

2.10 Flexibility in Managing a Culturally Challenging Situation: Sharing a Personal Experience in Dealing with Language Barriers – Allen Nankunda[29]

Providing services in a country with different customs, traditions and language can be challenging. Adapting oneself to the situation is very important in order to offer good services. Telling yourself "I can manage" helps to provide you all the determination needed to succeed. This case describes my experience as a consultant, and how I was able to overcome barriers to communication while developing a training package on Inter-personal Communication (IPC) and training trainers. This despite important discussions being conducted in a language I did not understand in spite of assurances beforehand that English would be the working language spoken and understood by all those involved.

I could not cite local examples because I was not familiar with the culture. To manage the situation, I had to be friendly, open and flexible. This meant I had to "adjust" my usual self in many ways. I discovered that a smile could help break barriers that may exist due to differences in culture, language and background. Establishing many "check points" for eliciting feedback was helpful in directing the way I dealt with barriers. In addition, late night "thinking" helped me devise strategies of moving on. I, together with the participants, looked forward to the next day even when we were aware that at some point they had to use the language they are familiar with. The key challenge was how to communicate effectively when there were differences in language and culture.

Understanding the Cultural Challenge

Most workshop participants wondered how I understood the local language despite being in the country for the first time. The five-week assignment I undertook could not offer adequate opportunity to learn the local language spoken by majority of the people with whom I interacted. I had to be flexible and creative so as to understand what was being communicated. Admittedly, sometimes my mind would "get lost" and "fly home", even when physically observing situations being acted out. But of course, I would quickly return to follow the

---

[29] Nankunda Babihuga A., Executive Director Communication for Development Foundation Uganda (CDFU) / Independent Consultant

discussions. On some occasions, the participants would ask: "Nankunda, how come you understand our language well? Have you been here before?" With a smile, I would say, "I can tell what has been discussed." I discovered that being confident would help me keep focused, even though understanding fully what was being communicated was sometimes difficult.

Even if cultures are different, all people desire to be respected. Therefore, they have to be given choice to communicate in a language they understand well. Language and the way a person communicates can affect the quality of work. Sometimes, the people being addressed may have physical impairments that affect the way they receive and perceive information. Utilizing experts in this field, such as those who use sign language, can help to ensure effective communication. It is important to learn how to express at least a few words, for example "greetings" and "thank you", in the language of the audience. In identifying the best way to communicate to a group, expressions or verbal communication have to be considered. Through sharing experiences and meals with the participants, I was able to break the barriers that may have existed and were likely to influence our interactions and hence affect the way I carried out the assignment.

Getting to the Country – A Totally New Environment
Although this country is in Africa, I had never visited it nor even interacted with anyone from there. It was a completely new experience for me. At the airport in a neighbouring country, the staff did not even know the airline I was booked on. This made me wonder how the experience would turn out and I asked myself: "Did I make the right decision in accepting this work?" During a long wait at the airport, I met a lady from Kenya who was also travelling to the same country. She was also a consultant and had spent three months in the country. She told me the "dos" and "don'ts", and this went a long way in preparing me for the eventualities. However, she did not tell me about the language issue.

Upon arrival, I was taken to a hotel near the office I was going to operate. The lady at the front desk asked for my passport so she could take my details as part of the "check in" process. I realized she wrote "M" on the form she was filling. When I asked what this meant, she said I was male! I was surprised that she could not tell from my voice that I was female. She said the confusion was because of my

short hair – in that country, all ladies have long hair. The officials I worked closely with were friendly and helped me adapt to the situation, regularly checking on whether or not I was coping.

The Challenging Task
Building the capacity of in-country partners can be both interesting and challenging, especially if you have to offer services among people who may not be speaking a language in which you are fluent. Relating well with the in-country teams is as important as the quality of the technical assistance delivered. Most of the time, the hosts are waiting to "test" whether you are capable of doing a good job or not. The weighting usually happens in the first rounds of meetings where decisions are made. You can hear comments like "We have had consultants that did not do much". This is a clear warning that they are watching every step!

How well you respect their culture is also critical. The experience in this case was unique because it involved working in an environment where the local language is widely spoken at school and at work. I had been informed that all participants for the training workshops could read and write English. During the teleconference I had with the in-country experts it was confirmed that English would be the language in use, which was reassuring for me at the time, so it came as a surprise later on when some participants made their contributions in the local language. Others even filled in the daily evaluations in the local language. I thought it was best to ask each one to use the language they were comfortable with, as this helped them to express themselves better.

Taking on the Challenge
Throughout the duration of the assignment, I had to try as far as possible to follow what was spoken in a language that was unknown to me. My eyes helped me to guess what was being discussed. As I gave my comments on the presentations and discussions, I used this opportunity to validate whether I had interpreted everything correctly. I had to keep alert at all times. Keeping eye contact with the audience helped me "guess" what was being described by observing the gestures of the speakers. I cannot remember any other time I have had to engage all of my senses so attentively.

Language 1-0-1
I decided that the language barrier would not deter me from doing a good job. For example, the woman who cleaned the training room did not know any English, yet she was the first person I interacted with every morning before the training started. As we rode back to office after the first day's session, I asked the driver and the official from the agency to teach me a few local words. I made some notes and kept referring to them. By the second day, I had learnt how to greet in the local language – my aim was to establish some relationship with those who would affect my work. That morning, I greeted the participants in the local language and they were happy about my effort.

Gestures and Eye Contact
The work involved developing a training package: "Training Package for Enhancing Interpersonal Communication Skills of Health Care Service Providers" and utilizing it to train trainers who would provide

country-wide trainings. The approaches used included utilization of existing materials to develop the content of the package, discussions with key stakeholders, particularly government departments, empowering the participants to lead the process by giving them opportunities to practise, and establishing good working relationships with in-country officials.

The workshops were highly participatory. Methods used included group discussions, role plays and analysis of case studies. PowerPoint presentations were only used to summarise key points and this was highly appreciated by the participants. I managed to capture the interest of the learners by involving them actively and referring to them by their names. Maintaining good eye contact with the learners helped to keep everyone alert. The diversity of the participants required good skills in retaining their interest and motivating them to participate in the learning process.

Having enough knowledge and experience helps in building confidence and in performing effectively. The training was highly participatory, providing all participants the opportunities to contribute. Each person was allowed to express themselves in the language they were comfortable with. However, this did not sit well with some participants who felt all interactions should be in English and expressed this in the daily evaluation. Allowing people to express themselves in a language they understood would help to maximize involvement. Most people value their cultures and language deeply. Many times I would imagine myself as a participant discussing in my local language as the facilitator struggled to understand what was taking place, and I wondered how I might handle the situation differently. Despite the difficulty, I was determined to overcome the challenges.

Processes *"Check Points"*
Beyond the usual techniques, I put in place many mechanisms for soliciting feedback. In addition to the "eye" and "ear" reports used to assess how the training was progressing, each day I asked two volunteers to observe the training, specifically the way I facilitated and whether I managed the sessions well. I held debriefing sessions with the observers every evening. My openness, flexibility and willingness to listen and learn encouraged the participants to provide honest feedback. This was why the participants felt I understood the language. The fact that they thought I understood them well stimu-

lated more interest in trying to "grab" the meanings of the words communicated. The discussions at the end of the day informed the "homework" I would do every night to make the next sessions even better. I was able to follow the discussions and made great effort to understand the expressions.

In addition, all participants filled out anonymous evaluation forms that I analyzed every evening. Each night, I spent hours thinking through how to make the next day more interesting. At the start of the day, we would discuss issues that were raised and this helped to clarify differences. For instance, some participants did not feel comfortable discussing female circumcision and we had to strike a balance between achieving our objective and being sensitive to people's cultures. There were diverse opinions among the participants themselves, even though many shared a common language. Making the sessions fascinating by involving the participants and making them laugh occasionally helped us forget about the cultural differences that existed.

Working with the in-country team
Working closely with the in-country team was very helpful. Most people were willing to assist. The team was supportive, open and willing to share information. The counterpart officials introduced me to key government officials, and this helped me become acquainted with what was needed beyond the Terms of Reference. Sometimes, the written terms may not fully articulate what is expected. For instance, I learned that I had to put more emphasis on skills building so the participants could facilitate trainings on their own. Being friendly and wearing a smile helped to establish an atmosphere of openness that was a critical element in bridging gaps.

Relating well with the stakeholders and respecting their views made life easier for me. They felt I was "one of them" and this helped to minimize the differences between us. Many of them asked if I could visit their families to learn more about their culture. I only managed to visit one home and it was a great learning experience that helped me bridge more gaps. I later discovered the visit contributed a lot to my strategies for overcoming challenges.

A Satisfying Result
Throughout the process, I focused on building capacity of the coun-

try partners to enable them to facilitate the trainings, and in the future, to update the IPC package as the need arises. The key gap had been skills development in training and this was effectively addressed through the use of adult learning methodologies, which ensured high levels of participation. A good trainer can apply any language and still be able to utilize skills that promote involvement of all participants.

Evaluation of the training showed that the participants rated the training highly. One participant indicated that he had not seen this kind of facilitation before. Participants appreciated the learner-centered approach of the training. Some noted that the facilitator was "tolerant" and "flexible". One participant found the facilitation "always warm". Another expressed that he had learned a lot from the facilitator; particularly being able to see all participants at all times (maintaining good eye contact).

By the end of the training workshops, most participants expressed that they were comfortable with facilitating sessions on IPC in their own language. Some had never facilitated trainings before, but the trial sessions helped them to become more confident. One participant said: "My expectations were highly fulfilled in the last five days. I liked the facilitation that was being used. I hope to apply it when facilitating other trainings."

Consultant capacity
I was able to transfer skills even though language was often a barrier. Utilizing simple language, and being open and friendly made my work easier. I am comfortable that the majority of the participants would go on to train others as shown in the trial sessions. What I did differently was to ask them to imagine real life situations during the practical sessions and to use their mother-tongue.

National teams' capacity
Feedback from the in-country experts, who reviewed the package, attended the trainings and from those who participated in the exit meeting indicated that they were happy with the outputs. Fifty-six participants including health workers, staff from the health education and promotion department, as well as other Ministry of Health officials, were trained to use the package. The trained participants are expected to roll out the training country-wide.

A good consultant has to be flexible to fit the circumstances, which are always different. Respect for all people and establishment of good interpersonal relationships is an important aspect in creating an enabling environment for offering effective capacity building services. In-country teams have different attitudes towards assistance being offered by consultants, as they sometimes feel it is not worth the value. Effectively delivery in these contexts may sometimes mean going "out of one's way" to add value, irrespective of the barriers that may arise.

Key points:
- Being knowledgeable in the topic of discussion is critical.
- Keeping high spirits and interest in the work by the consultant helps to motivate the in-country teams.
- Flexibility and good listening skills enable the consultant to maintain good relationships with all stakeholders.
- Utilization of participatory and adult learning techniques ensures involvement of all participants, thus motivating interest in the training.
- Participatory techniques also help to minimize barriers to communication.
- Putting in place as many methods as possible to obtain feedback improves outcomes.
- Being friendly and open helps to capture all discussions and encourages forward movement, even when there are differences in language and culture.
- A good consultant has to be sensitive to people's cultures and knowing how to adjust to unique situations is a key to overcoming barriers to communication.

2.11 Even a long journey starts with a small step: Reflections on technical support including Community System Strengthening in the Global Fund HIV Plan for China - Zhai Wen[30]

Community participation is often equated with program success and sustainability. In the Global Fund (GF) HIV work in China, community-based organizations (CBOs) do participate but their involvement is limited. Issues such as the lack of an enabling and supporting environment, weak organizational capacities and inadequate resources are some of the most persistent barriers to participation.

These issues constitute a vicious cycle which hinders CBO participation and thus obstructs meaningful contribution to the GF and to HIV work as a whole in China. One way to break the vicious cycle would be to strengthen CBOs to enable them to contribute consistently towards a more efficient and effective approach through GF resources. The inclusion of a community system strengthening (CSS) component in the GF Rolling Continuation Channel (RCC) HIV proposal might be a viable and strategic initiative. This paper elaborates and reflects on the processes in achieving such an inclusion.

The journey starts here

China's political, cultural, social and historical attributes set the country in a unique context. Having come into shape only in recent years, CBOs are now the most common institutional form in China and their participation has been recognized as an indispensable element in any HIV program.

As argued by a local CBO representative, *"the participation of CBOs in GF programs is crucial in realizing the services provided to each targeted individual"* (Zhai Wen, 2008[31]). This is echoed by a UNAIDS expert, who stated that the response to HIV can only be effective with community participation, as governments could only go so far[32].

---

[30] Zhai Wen, Independent Consultant
[31] Zhai Wen, 2008. Survey among 25 community-based organization on Community system strengthening in the Global Fund
[32] Schwartländer, B. 2008. Bringing the response to where the epidemic is happening – presentation in Hong Kong.

As one of the largest HIV-related funds operating in China, the Global Fund recognizes community participation as a crucial strategy for its effectiveness. It is a potential platform to facilitate more meaningful and sustainable participation of CBOs. However, even if it has invested a great deal of effort towards such a direction, issues are increasingly raised by researchers and communities that CBO involvement is far from satisfactory, especially in the field of AIDS.

At its best, according to a sub-sub-recipient (SSR) CBO representative, *"we are merely completing the jobs that government assigned us to do, without knowing clearly our identity and what we are actually doing"* (Zhai Wen, 2008).

Based on two surveys conducted in 2008 by Zhai Wen and the non-governmental organization section of China Global Fund country coordination mechanism (CCM) respectively, a few prominent issues exist as barriers to the participation of CBOs in Global Fund HIV related disease work.

There has not been a specific component dedicated to CBO participation in the previous China's GF HIV plans. As a result, even if CBOs do participate in GF work, their involvement is highly constrained within the directions of government in a '*do as told*' manner. For the most part, funds provided to CBOs for capacity building efforts are directed towards activity implementation and not to organizational development. There is also competition between the semi-governmental and non-governmental organizations. As put by a representative from a CBO supporting HIV-affected children, *"GF does not make clear categorization between grassroots CBOs and government- organised NGOs (GONGOs)[33], and the latter have taken a great proportion of GF resources"* (Zhai Wen, 2008).

The contrast between the universal recognition of the essentiality of community participation in HIV work and the pervasive unsatisfactory reality makes it urgent and crucial to facilitate efforts to strengthen community involvement in GF HIV work in China.

---

[33] GONGOs refer to the organisations organised and closely monitored by government agencies, while in their legal/registration status they are not-for-profit and non-government organizations. This is a characteristically unique type of organisation whose nature only overlaps partially with the NGOs as described and interpreted internationally.

> **What is the Global Fund (GF)?**
> The Global Fund is a unique global public/private partnership dedicated to attracting and disbursing additional resources to prevent and treat HIV, tuberculosis and malaria. Since its creation in 2002, the GF has become the main fund source for programs to fight AIDS, tuberculosis and malaria, with approved funding of US$ 15.6 billion for more than 572 programs in 140 countries. It provides a quarter of all international financing for AIDS globally, two-thirds for tuberculosis and three quarters for malaria. (The Global Fund, 2009a)

Getting ready for the journey

In October 2008, a TSF (HIV and AIDS Technical Support Facility) consultant, together with two other participants from China - one from a local grassroots CBO and the other from GF Country Coordination Mechanism People Living with HIV (PLHIV) section - participated in a workshop on Community System Strengthening (CSS). The workshop aimed to introduce CSS as a concept and advocate the possibility of its inclusion in Global Fund proposals.

> **What is Community System Strengthening?** (The Global Fund, 2009b)
> As a proposed concept, CSS embraces the following aspects:
> 1. Building capacity of CBOs (including physical infrastructure, communication technology, financial management, strategic planning capacity, Monitoring and Evaluation and information management capacity;
> 2. Building partnership at the local level to improve coordination; enhancing impact and avoiding duplication of service delivery; and
> 3. Sustainable long-term financing of CBOs.

Including CSS in China's upcoming GF RCC HIV proposal was not an easy decision to take. On one hand, the China delegates were thinking about several challenges: the limited time available to develop the proposal, competition over the available funds, and the fact that the CSS concept was new to China, with a low level of understanding existing among government and non-government organizations in this regard. On the other hand, the group felt that the necessary assets to reconcile most disadvantages were accessible. The TSF consultant had experience in advocacy and had worked with and for local CBOs on HIV in China, while the CCM PLHIV representative had extensive contacts with other CCM members and some international donors in China. The CBO participant worked in a sub-sub-recipient (SSR) organisation in China. So, within a short period, he was able to help the TSF consultant to understand their involvement and the general sentiments among fellow CBOs towards GF. Additionally, the CSS Regional Consultant, who was also a facilitator at the workshop, had been involved in GF writing for a few years and he was invited again by China CCM to assist the RCC HIV proposal writing group. By doing so, he would also have direct access to the core group of people who would be developing the HIV proposal.

After weighing up their options, the participants from China decided that CSS was a valuable and crucial initiative to be included in the forthcoming China GF RCC HIV proposal. Towards the end of the workshop, they reached consensus to work on the CSS inclusion and to commit themselves to contribute to the process. Meanwhile, the TSF consultant agreed to become the National Consultant for this particular task. At the end of the workshop, the national consultant, together with the other colleagues, prepared a schedule for the consultancy task which was later agreed by the other participants. Specific roles for each individual, including the Regional Consultant, were identified.

Making a roadmap and Go!
Processes in this consultancy were executed in three main steps. Firstly, interested parties were identified through existing networks of the CSS workshop participants. Secondly, they also disseminated a brief paper on CSS to potential groups and individuals. It was hoped that these groups and individuals would later endorse CSS within their scope of influence. Thirdly, the proposals and other materials to be used were 'brewed' through a consultation meeting with 25 CBOs, which were either existing SSRs in GF HIV, or interested in becoming one. Fourthly, the requests and suggestions on CSS from the 25 CBOs, other groups and individuals were expressed in a concerted manner officially and publicly.

Before eliciting views on issues and recommendations related to CBO participation in GF, accurate understanding on CSS was ensured by disseminating a briefing paper through the email groups in the CCM NGO and PLHIV sections. An introduction to CSS was also attached to the survey questionnaires distributed to participating CBOs. During the course of responding to the CSS, the national consultant was available through email and phone communications for clarification.

Table 1: Strategies and Steps for CSS Inclusion Consultancy in China

Activities	Target	By Whom
1 Preparations: **Who will be standing with us?**	• Potentially interested groups and individuals	National consultant with support from CSS other workshop participants and RC
2 Consultation and endorsement mobilizations: **What should we propose?** ▪ Conceptualisation ▪ Survey ▪ Other consultations	• Local CBOs	National consultant with support from CCM members
3 Proposal development	• CCM	National consultant with support from RC
4 Case presentation: **By whom and how it will be heard?** ▪ Endorsement expansion ▪ Open petition	• CCM	NGO and PLHIV CCM members, with support from RC and NC

It was crucial to present the concept to relevant government agencies, so that political sensitivities were minimized and readiness in accepting it was enhanced. The Regional Consultant provided a briefing through a PowerPoint presentation to facilitate understanding of CSS among government officials at the national level, and the document was subsequently forwarded to other departments.

Twenty-five CBOs participated in the survey on CSS in GF work. The collected issues and recommendations raised were later analyzed and summarized by the national consultant in a proposal, which was submitted to the China CCM Secretariat prior to the start of the writing process. Parallel to the proposal, two open letters were issued by the PLHIV and NGO sections to request serious consideration of the proposal from the CCM Secretariat.

Most of the issues and recommendations identified by the 25 CBOs and included in the proposal were in line with the CSS as a generic concept but adapted to the context of China. A Men-Who-Have-Sex-With-Men (MSM) CBO representative said, *"The previously loose and simple organizational structure will not be able to meet the demands (from GF HIV work). Personnel capacity, allocation and management of resources and quality of program implementation are all affected*".

This was supported by comments made by an IDU group member: *"The level of difficulty in our work has been growing. Opportunities of renewing knowledge and respective funds should be more channelled to grassroots organisations. The GF funds are largely managed in CDCs and government HIV offices thus only a little is being given to grassroots NGOs and CBOs. This poses challenges to their program implementation work, which will be hard to be in-depth"*.

Similar comments on lack of support pointed to a negative impact on CBO sustainability, about which a CBO representative pointed out the "*absence of salary support that makes the grassroots CBOs largely volunteer-based*" can result in a serious problem of loss of CBO core members. An MSM group representative suggested that "*GF should support CBOs to have independent office space and basic equipment, so their members can work in the same location*" thereby strengthening efficacy, team spirit and capacity.

In terms of funding sustainability, a sex worker support group member said: *"Support with sustainable funds is essential"*, and *"funds should not only be targeted at activity but also the long-term development of organizations"*.

Regarding communication and consultation within the GF system and between government and CBOs, a CBO representative suggested that: *"A broader consultation system should be established with CBOs and should not be limited to 'experts'"*.

In late November, the first draft of the China RCC HIV proposal was developed and sent out to all CCM members for comments. This document included a section of five supporting documents, of which four were closely linked to CSS and adapted from the CSS proposal, and open letters put forward to the CCM Secretariat.

It is therefore evident that the China CCM, during the processes of proposal development, did give careful consideration to the issues and recommendations raised. Even though political sensitivities precluded some of the documents being incorporated the final version as a separate annex, their inclusion in the early version clearly had an important impact during the process of writing and finalisation of the proposal.

Taking a small step forward

The most encouraging result from the consultancy efforts is the incorporation of CSS in most aspects of the final RCC proposal and a separate Service Delivery Area (SDA) dedicated to CSS. Community participation is incorporated in most of these SDAs, particularly under the first objective which reads as: "*CSS: strengthening of institutional and civil society capacity*".

> The China RCC HIV proposal has the goal of *'scaling up HIV prevention, treatment and care in China to achieve universal access'*, under which four objectives are included.
> 1. Strengthen the supporting environment to ensure universal access to HIV prevention, treatment, care and support services for target populations
> 2. Increase coverage and quality of comprehensive HIV prevention programs for key populations at higher risk of HIV (Female Sex Workers, MSM and IDU) and PMTCT
> 3. Increase access and quality of treatment, care and support and secondary prevention services for PLHIV
> 4. Information and program management

SDA 1.4 included specific CSS-related activities such as:
- Develop a sustainable financial and program management structure for funding NGO/CBO activities and institutional development.
- Strengthen NGO/CBO capacity in planning, management and service delivery in line with national and local policies; and,
- Establish NGO partnerships and communication/coordination mechanisms at local levels and ensure linkages with multi-sectoral working mechanisms.

The CSS SDA responds to many issues and incorporates recommendations raised by CBOs in the CSS proposal. Capacity building for CBOs and NGOs is planned for, including both project management and organizational development. Funding support has been specified for basic operational costs of CBOs. It was emphasised that funding support for overhead costs for CBOs was urgently needed to ensure their sustainable and meaningful contribution. A longer-term NGO/

CBO-led capacity building approach was given emphasis. Communication for CBOs is addressed by stating that *'the innovative NGO Advisory Group and Consulting Group mechanisms created under GF5 and 6'* should be continued and expanded, together with the establishment of an exchange and sharing platform particularly for participating CBOs and NGOs.

Another major achievement is the Funding allocation of CSS component. The Technical Review Panel (TRP) of GF[34] preliminarily approved a budget of USD 1,761,600 dollars under the CSS (SDA 1.4) section. This subtotal amount is the 11th largest out of the 20 SDAs in the proposal. Although its proportion may look small compared to the overall funding requested (USD 497 million), at least now it has a significant and dedicated funding allocation as compared to the past arrangement where funding for NGOs has often been blurred with funding for Government-NGOs (GONGOs) or other vague categories.

It is believed that by the end of the consultancy project, the level and depth of understanding on CSS amongst relevant stakeholders, especially CBOs, had been strengthened. Coherence between CSS as a concept and issues and recommendations made by the involved CBOs proves this outcome. This in turn facilitates the strengthening of self-esteem among CBOs as a whole, by openly recognizing their important positions and roles in Global Fund and other HIV work. While their expertise, experience and skills are usually questioned by others, the increase in self-confidence helps local CBOs, particularly small and grassroots ones, to maintain an enthusiastic spirit and encourages them to make further contributions to HIV work.

Looking back at the road
Reflecting on the experience, many lessons can be learned from the consultancy process and the required conditions that promote participation of CBOs, particularly in HIV related disease work.

The Consultancy Processes
This experience provides a familiar scenario of many consultants: limitations in resources, time, experience and other barriers. In order

---

[34] As per communication between GF TRP and the applicant country's GF CCM in March 2009, the proposal was approved for its funding for the first 3 years.

to maximize the outputs and outcomes, it is important to mobilize possible support as well as facilitate the use of experience and resources at hand. The pairing of a regional and national consultant has resulted in complementary expertise. Using a local consultant is a strategic approach in facilitating and mobilizing supporting factors and resources, in a context often unfamiliar to expatriate consultants.

Participating in workshops and meetings not only builds the technical capacity of consultants, in this case, strengthening understanding of CSS, but also provides opportunities to work with a group of like-minded people and build networks with local and international colleagues who can later be part of a valuable resource.

The Basics

The experience brought forth a realization that to achieve sustainable and meaningful participation of CBOs in the GF in China, there are fundamental principles that need to be established. Certain issues have to be confronted and addressed; otherwise CSS will not be recognized and realized in GF and other HIV projects. Indeed, changes made to the CSS component between the earlier and final versions of the proposal reflect that there are still reservations in understanding the significance and urgency of CSS.

First of all, the CBO understanding on the structure of Global Fund projects needs to be improved, as this greatly hinders their capacity in discussing and raising issues, as well as in making recommendations and suggestions for GF in China. Without a good understanding of its system, it would be challenging for CBO to find ways to participate, not to mention contribute to GF work.

Secondly, the issue of CBO legitimacy in China has to be dealt with. As elaborated in the RCC Proposal, many of the CBOs, especially the nascent ones, are either unregistered or registered as a non-NGO entity e.g. as a business. There is simply a lack of channels, referable standardized regulations and procedures for registration. However, changes have emerged in the last year[35].

---

[35] For example, in one province, the Provincial Bureau of Civil Affairs revised the Registration Management Regulation for Social Groups, which made it possible for small CBOs (those with only one staff member can register) to operate in a legal way. This could be a special case, but it could also be a sign of broader national change.

Thirdly, it is important for the CBOs to understand that collaboration, communication and sharing are more important than competition at this stage. Only through collaboration can a louder and more concerted voice be created and heard to make structural change towards a more enabling environment for healthy civil society development in China. This concern needs to be directed towards the development of a more transparent, democratic and open application and management structure for GF projects. It is worth noting that Monitoring and Evaluation is another field that the Proposal prioritizes. Jointly, these efforts will help to strengthen the credibility and accountability of CBOs as a whole.

Steps ahead
As the Taoist Lao Tse said, "The journey of a thousand miles begins with one step". The inclusion of CSS in China's Global Fund RCC HIV proposal is one of these small steps which can lead to changes in the asymmetrical power relationship that predominantly prevents CBOs from meaningful and sustainable participation in programs like those of the GF.

Experience from this particular consultancy reflects that a paradigm shift can start with small changes achieved through inputs from short term technical support. Such small changes should not be judged by how much funding they can bring to the tens of thousands of CBOs in China. It can become a start of a systemic transition. As consultants, our job is to consider how to facilitate this transition with our long-term commitment to contributing our technical expertise, with support from like-minded people and a strategy contextualised in the right time and the right place.

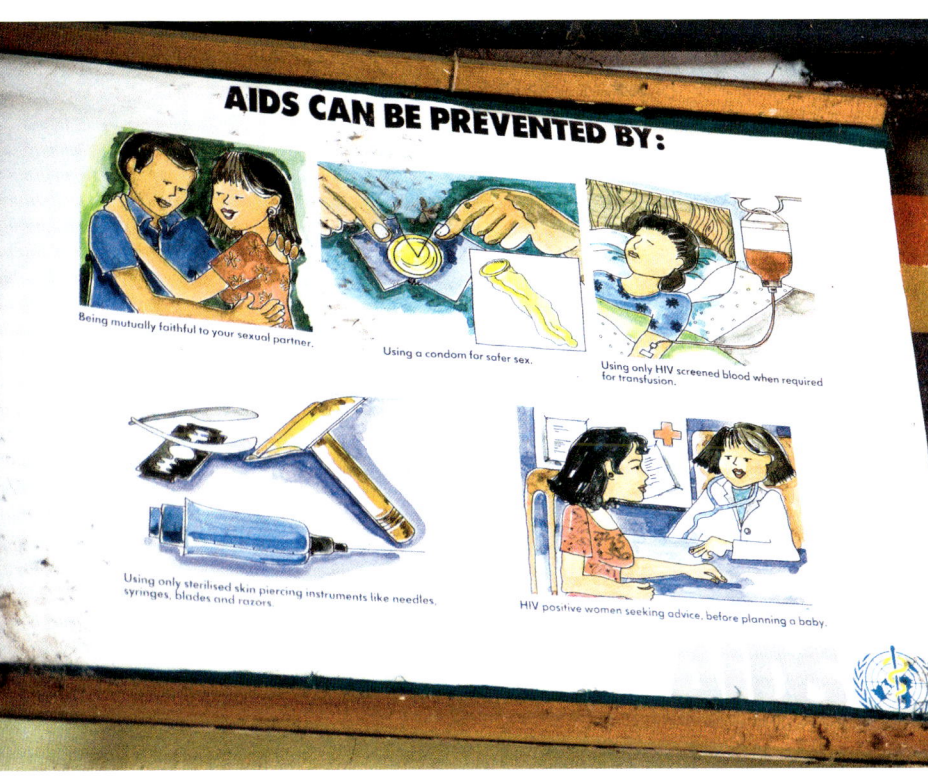

Chapter 3:
Experiences in Technical Assistance

Technical Assistance (TA) is a critical component of any intervention on AIDS. Organizations implementing programs and initiatives are unlikely to have all the knowledge, skills and resources internally to be able to effectively implement their initiatives. TA helps to fill the gaps. The TA process can involve multiple stakeholders taking on specific roles: the TA recipient who has a need for TA; the TA provider who fulfils this need; the TA manager who coordinates and administers the TA between the stakeholders; and the TA funder who provides the financial resources.

A TA assignment follows a life-cycle that has a series of stages, each with its own processes and challenges. Roles and responsibilities of stakeholders differ across the stages. A successful TA is one that is useful to the recipient. It offers a learning and satisfactory experience for the provider. It runs smoothly and provides value for money to the funder.

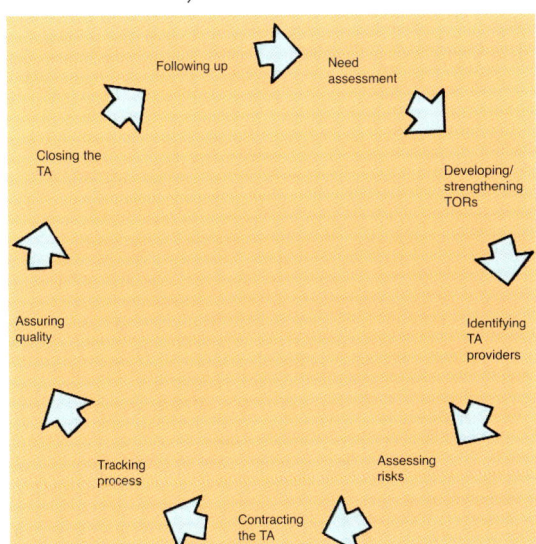

The Life Cycle of Technical Assistance

This section presents three case studies on TA management. The first paper "*In Unison – Good practices in TA management*" (3.1) traces the experiences and challenges of four persons in receiving, providing and managing TA. These varied experiences across the TA life-cycle serve to draw key learning that would benefit all stakeholders in optimal management of the TA process.

Focusing on specific experiences from West and Central Africa, the second paper, "*Responding to the HIV epidemic in West and Central Africa: Managing Technical Assistance*" (3.2), shows that TA provision is not an easy task. It requires understanding the country partner's needs, matching quality TA services to these needs, and learning from TA activities to better respond to future needs. The paper also illustrates how a comprehensive program that integrates TA and Capacity Development can improve the delivery of a country's response to the epidemic.

Irrespective of management paradigms, sometimes circumstances that emerge do not allow for ideal processes or detailed planning. An attractive opportunity or undue pressure from higher quarters may be difficult to ignore. In such conditions the risks of failure or compromised quality are increased. The third paper, "*Mission Impossible: Delivering quality outputs within a short time*" (3.3) presents a case where normal processes had to be bypassed given time pressure. While there is recognition that such situations should be avoided as much as possible, the case shows that given the right resources, the technical assistance may still turn out to be timely and acceptable to the client.

3.1 In Unison: Good Practices in TA Management – Siddhi Mankad[36]

Technical assistance (TA) is component of project planning and execution that – if provided and utilized well - can add significant value to an initiative. This paper draws from amongst others the experiences of Reena, James and Deepak, three TA managers from the Technical Support Facilities (TSFs) and Swasti, a health resource centre, in managing, providing and utilizing TA. It highlights good practices in TA management across the TA life cycle. It takes a 360-degree view of TA from the perspectives of a TA recipient, a TA provider and a TA manager.

"This time, Reena knew she had to be careful. She sat her consultant down and gave a detailed briefing on the assignment. Together they developed a plan on the task ahead. They agreed that he would keep sending her chapters of the document as he completed writing them so that she could provide feedback in a focused and staggered manner, rather than do a last-minute rush through reams of pages. This time, the consultancy would work for all – the client, the consultant and for herself".

[36] Siddhi Mankad – Swasti health resource centre, India

The TA process has diverse "players" with distinct and overlapping roles that need to work harmoniously to ensure concerted action and unison to satisfy the needs of all. Successful TA management draws on a wide range of skills, from project management, human resource management and stakeholder management to problem-solving and communication.

Reena explains the necessity for TA: "As project manager of a learning systems project, I had to build technical assistance into the proposal. The project focused on capacity development, research and documentation to capture and disseminate learning on HIV prevention initiatives in the Karnataka state of India. The scope of work required such diverse skills and expertise at different periods in the course of the project that it would be impossible to recruit as many people within the project. TA was the strategy to acquire resources and expertise according to needs in order to ensure the best possible output. In addition to augmenting internal skills and capacities, TA assignments also address the need for neutrality or an external perspective, as in the case of program reviews."

Box 1: Stakeholders in the TA process
- The TA recipient: the person or institution with a need for TA to address a gap in skills, capacities, knowledge or resources.
- The TA provider: the person or institution with skills, capacities, knowledge to address these gaps through consultancy services.
- The TA funder: an organization that bears the cost of the TA provided to the recipient, to enable the latter to source critical inputs that it may not otherwise be able to afford.
- The TA manager: the person coordinating between the recipient, provider and funder to ensure efficient TA provision. The TA manager has access to a pool of consultants in diverse practice areas and ensures quality control of the TA process. The TA manager can identified from within the recipient organization, or from a TA management agency such as the TSF.

Identifying the Need for TA

Need is the operative word here. TA management begins with assessing the need for TA. James, a TSF TA manager shares an interesting experience. *"We've recently got a request from a national AIDS program to develop a Civil Service Organization's operational manual. A similar manual has already been developed in another region and can be adapted within the national program. We do not feel it is judicious to use funds to 're-invent the wheel'. This is a tricky situation. As a TA manager, it is my responsibility to advise the program on effective TA utilization. Yet, TSF is committed to supporting the TA needs demanded by national programs. I have written to concerned persons about re-visiting the need for TA in this area and working with available documents."*

Deepak, a TA manager, recalls one of his first experiences in hiring a consultant. *"The deliverable was a process documentation that needed to be outsourced, given the absence of a documentation officer. The project manager and I were unclear as to its value to the project. We ended up choosing the wrong consultant for the job and not providing her with clear direction, support and feedback. In the end, we got 150 pages of structured notes. We closed the consultancy. And though the document came in handy – with information flowing in bits and pieces into the annual report and a review exercise - we did not get the process document we'd required."*

Box 2: The need to have a need
- Articulation of need enables:
- A decision on whether or not the TA is required
- Assessment of whether or not it needs to be outsourced
- Planning and budgeting – keeping in mind the scope
- Identification of the right consultant/s
- Focused feedback
- Execution of quality processes and outputs

These experiences remind us that if the need for TA is not identified at the outset, there is a greater risk of problems emerging during the course of the TA, or of the TA not culminating in useful outputs.

Developing/Strengthening the TORs

The TOR is the window to the TA. It communicates not only the TA requirements and expectations, but also generates interest among the right kind of prospective consultants. The TOR is the basis on which the consultant plans the methodologies, activities, resource requirements and timelines, and develops the budget.

"There was one TOR where the client wanted the whole world, and then some more", Preeti, a consultant, laughingly recalls. *"They wanted to do a review and a capacity building needs assessment (CBNA), all through a single contract. We dialogued with them and explained that the review would provide the pointers that would feed into the*

> **Box 3: Importance of TORs**
> TORs flow from the need of the TA. They need to be tightly focused to provide a background and context to the TA, elucidate the scope and expected deliverables, outline expected processes, suggest budget limits if possible, and provide contacts for applicants to seek clarification. Focused TORs provide:
> - Clarity to all stakeholders on expectations
> - Basis for risk assessment
> - Basis for development of the execution and progress tracking plan

CBNA. Besides, the skills and expertise, timelines and tasks differed between the two outputs and it would not be possible for us to do both together. They saw our point and dropped the latter from the TOR."

James is of the opinion that if possible, all stakeholders should be involved in the finalization of the TORs. *"Dialogue between the TA recipients, funders, providers and managers facilitates common understanding on the deliverables and expectations."*

Identifying the TA Providers

After finalizing the TOR, a TA manager needs to find the right consultant. TA managers are usually familiar with a number of consultants, or have access to databases from whence they can source new names. James is an old hand at this. *"I prefer working with consultants who have delivered good services in the past or who come highly recommended from friends and colleagues. Usually when I get a request for TA – even as I read through the draft TORs - I am searching my mental database for suitable consultants."*

The dilemma in TA management is whether to refer known consultants to the client, or to identify new ones. Using known consultants provides a sense of security and reduces the effort in managing the TA. But a safe option is not always the best option. By using the same consultants frequently the pool of reliable consultants shrinks. If known consultants are not available to attend to requests for critical pieces of work, using 'first-time' consultants may be risky. Known consultants may also not be able to bring in new or fresh perspectives. By not scouting for new consultants, the TA manager risks not having consultants with better or different abilities on hand.

Box 4: Ways to assess risk

Once a TOR is received, a short exercise is carried out to categorize assignments A, B or C.

There are two broad approaches to adopt for risk analysis and categorization:

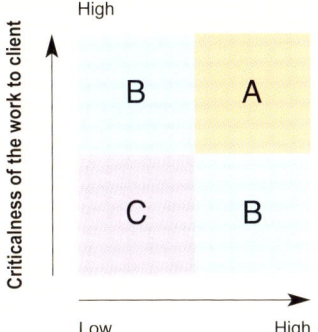

Another methodology of risk analysis is to identify risks of failure across some of the key and known parameters:

Risk of problems / failure

No	Risk	High	Medium	Low
1	New and untested consultant			
2	New context / country for the consultant			
3	Difficult client to please (past experience)			
4	Initial indicators that the context is hostile / unfriendly in some key quarters			
5	Assignment is of interest to a variety of stakeholders			
6	Assignment process or output is a crucial input for the client			
7	The process is long or political or both			

If a risk is high, a scoring of 10 is given; if medium, it is 5 and if low, it is 1. If the total is between 45-70, the assignment is categorized as A, between 21-44 as B and up to 20 as Category C.

Once the categorization is complete, then the quality assurance process varies depending on

The identification process should be varied on a case-to-case basis. When time is short or the assignment is critical to the client, known consultants are the best bet. For simpler assignments, it may be better to use new consultants who could be added to an ever-widening pool of known consultants. However, it is imperative that the TA manager does a thorough check on the candidate's references and a quality assessment of similar work done before commissioning a first-time consultant.

Assessing Risks
Before execution, it is useful to assess the risk level of the TA. Deepak explains: *"We grade an assignment based on how critical the assignment is to the recipient, and the risk of problems emerging. A TA with greater risk needs greater rigor in all processes of recruitment, progress tracking and quality control, thus requiring more time and effort. However, if the risk is low, we can calibrate our involvement and support downward. For instance, a country proposal is critical for the country program and we cannot afford delays or quality lapses. We employ senior resources and ensure constant tracking and communication with all stakeholders. A workshop, on the other hand, would not demand as much effort."*

The risk assessment should consider the type of client, experience of the consultant, experience of the TA manager, country/region of work and the associated socio-political environment, and any other factors that could have a significant bearing on the consultancy.

Contracting the TA
The contract seals the agreement between the consultant and the client. Preeti expressed some worries in this regard: *"Often the tasks are 'evolving' in nature, or cannot be accurately budgeted for in terms of time and timelines, as in the case of writing large funding proposals involving a number of consortium partners. While the deliverables are clear, the processes and efforts are not standard and depend on the capacities of the partners to align their proposal to the larger strategy. Some partners need more facilitation than others. Sometimes changes mid-way require rewriting, adding to the time and costs. Unless I get paid on actual time spent, I lose out."*

Deepak understands these concerns. *"Contracts are a critical component of employing TA. However, they are never carved in stone and flexibility can be built into them. Consultants should be fairly compensated for the value that they provide. In some assignments, time and budget increases are accepted by the client based on changes in the scope or unforeseen problems. But sometimes budgets are tight. If consultants are unable to agree to an expanded scope, the TA becomes less than successful. Many, however, do provide a service beyond the contract specifics, with passion and commitment to provide a 'TOR+', sensitivity to the needs of the client, and awareness that an expanded scope is a learning opportunity or can offer future work or favorable references."*

Preeti notes another angle to contracting. *"Some agencies add penalty clauses to the contract – cutting a percentage of the fees for late delivery. This keeps us focused and on our toes. If there is any possibility for slippages, we ensure that it is communicated to the client and approved in writing. I feel this is a good practice while contracting. However, I would be happier if there were also penalties suggested for failure of the recipient or client to adhere to their responsibilities."*

Tracking Progress
Progress tracking helps in managing the scope, time and quality of the TA. Periodic, at times even daily, tracking can flag emerging problems that can be addressed in time. Each stakeholder needs to tune these interactions and improvise. A "one size fits all" strategy will not work.

Effective tracking requires a plan for execution of the TA, which provides directions on how the TA will be tracked (through written reports, periodic progress reviews, and the like). The plan should detail the roles of all the parties and milestones against which progress is measured. *"In one assignment, the client was not providing timely feedback. When provided, it would comprise of diverse, even contradictory comments. Depending on the time and duration of the consultancy, it is recommendable to have a group or individual at the user organization that can collect feedback from all role players and distil it to provide one-point feedback and ensure quality control,"* explains Deepak. Preeti, the consultant, admits: *"Often, the interest and involvement of the client makes a difference on how we execute the consultancy. An involved client is usually a pleasure to work for, although at times, too much involvement can constrain our creativity. I feel that*

> **Box 5: Basis of the progress tracking plan**
> The level of engagement suggested by progress tracking will depend on:
> - The complexity and value of the assignment: difficult assignments or those of high value require intensive tracking
> - The identified consultants: known and more experienced may require lesser tracking
> - Capacity of the client to manage TA: clients who have had little experience in managing TA may require more support from the TA manager.

involvement of the client helps build their internal capacity. But this too has to be tempered, and should not get in the way of the execution of the TA. In one assignment, our client wanted to be so involved for his own learning that we usually ended up taking far longer for each activity than if we had worked independently."

Assuring Quality

Quality assurance (QA) cuts across all the phases of the TA life-cycle, ensuring that the outcomes of the TA meet its needs. It involves processes for correct identification of consultants, quality review of the deliverables, and constructive feedback – in the course of and at the end of the consultancy.

When QA processes are followed, the risks of disharmony are reduced, but there is no guarantee that a TA will always be successful. *"We should recognize that some consultancies will fail for a variety of reasons. While we cannot prevent this, we can only mitigate the effects by catching and addressing problems early on,"* notes Deepak. James adds: *"Defining quality is a tricky affair and quite variable. It needs to be understood at the outset. Communication, feedback and follow-up is the best way to keep track of quality in the course of the TA."*

Deepak recalls an assignment against which the consultant did not deliver a quality output. *"We were in a dilemma as to what to do. It is difficult to look at the situation dispassionately – to assess where the consultant failed, or where we failed in providing support. Ultimately, I felt responsible for the deliverable and re-worked the report to the best of my ability. We paid the consultant the full fees, but decided not to use him again."* Such "repairs" of the consultant's work by TA managers is not a desirable practice. By doing so, they absolve the consultant of poor-quality outputs, it is not a prudent use of the funds, and they also do the consultant harm by not giving him or her an opportunity to learn from mistakes. It may also be more costly than ending the contract mid-way. Breaking the consultancy into phases, with incremental payment processes based on phased deliverables, is a good method of tracking progress and cutting losses. Deepak cautions: *"Closing a consultancy mid-way is difficult. The TA manager needs assertiveness skills since most people do not like confrontations. The TA manager should keep a professional distance from the consultants, as getting too friendly may be an obstacle to giving adverse feedback. However, even when we change a consultant mid-way, we need to end the consultancy professionally. Recognize and respect that the consultant has capacities in other areas, so it is best to part on a pleasant note."*

James describes a case where consultants and TA managers was caught amid conflicts of interest between the funder and recipient agency. *"A large international donor agency wanted the national ministry of health to engage in a TA. The latter was unable to refuse for fear of jeopardizing funding of other programs. While the donor controlled the payment for the TA, the recipient controlled its process. The consultant sat in the recipient office, but received instructions from the donor. It was nightmarish for the consultant."*

Conflict of interests between the funder and recipient agency can be prevented by a clear definition of roles and establishing the engagement and expectations at the outset. Is the funder willing or expected to provide technical back-stopping support? What is the recipient's role in activities such as consultant identification, or appointment of members to a technical team? Who facilitates the TA? *"Where relationships are delicate, it is imperative that the stakeholders agree on common ground and establish responsibilities, deliverables and management processes,"* suggests James. *"And the TA manager is well-placed to facilitate this process."* However, during the course of the consultancy, all stakeholders also need to be alert to situations veering towards conflict, and to establish processes for timely resolution.

Closing the TA
Finally, the last stage of TA management arises – the closure. A critical closure process is the sign-off. Reena understands the importance

of the sign-off. *"I sign off on the TA to communicate that I have looked at the deliverables and find that they are of good quality, they meet the expectations laid down in the TORs, and that I can approve the release of final payments to the consultant who then bears no responsibility for any future objections to the deliverables. This also implies that I have ensured that the outputs have been shared with others within the project for whom the TA work has implications."* Sign-off is required from the recipient, the funder, the TA manager and a technical person in case the former are not capable of QA on the content.

With sign-off, internal closure processes are activated. A sound closure of the TA includes feedback between all the parties, putting together all the deliverables – reports, presentations, tools – and making them accessible at a central point, rating the consultant for future reference, and updating databases if required. This tends to be one of the most ignored phases of a TA. Deepak explains: *"Once the TA has been executed and the last deliverable satisfactorily provided, we tend to move on to the next assignment without completing all closure processes properly. We also face problems from the clients, who do not want to take time to provide feedback."* While it may be difficult to get feedback from the client or consultant, the TA manager needs to persist, or build it into the agreement. *"Written feedback is sometimes limiting, or the clients may not be comfortable being forthright on a feedback form. We find it useful sometimes to pick up the phone and get detailed feedback,"* says Deepak.

At the end of the TA the recipient, funder and management agencies could share their experiences and draw lessons on what to do and what not to do for improved management of future assignments.

Following-up

"Closure is not really the final step of TA," opines James. *"We need to do follow-up on the TAs. We should track how the work has benefited the client and communicate it back to all the stakeholders. This will give them learning for the future on the kinds of assignments to support and the processes thereof. Even if the TA has not been of use, it can contribute to informing future design. The recipient may also proactively inform the other stakeholders on the benefits of the support they have received. Follow-up usually never happens, since we have moved on to other work, but is a logical last step in the TA management process,"* he asserts.

Key lessons learned

James, Deepak, Preeti and Reena's experiences, although set within their own work context, provide universal learning for achieving unison in TA management among all stakeholders in the TA process. Key lessons learned from these experiences are:

1 It is important to deliberate and gain clarity on the need for the TA before deciding on commissioning it. Ensure that it is indeed required by the organization, and that internal resources do not exist to address the need. Ensure that the TORs articulate and address this need. TA managers could advise the recipient on this process.
2 Make use of opportunities to identify new consultants who can be added to the pool of known consultants.
3 Always assess the risk of the TA failing and calibrate management processes to prevent or reduce the risk. Be alert to emerging problems during the course of the assignment for timely resolution.
4 Prepare for the TA by establishing responsibilities, deliverables and management processes among all the stakeholders. Ensure that progress tracking covers all the three areas.
5 Ensure all stakeholders sign-off on the final deliverables for adherence to TORs and quality parameters.
6 Follow-up with the recipient after a while to determine whether and how they have benefited from the TA.

3.2 Responding to the HIV Epidemic in West and Central Africa: Managing Technical Assistance – Yvonne Ouattara[37]

Technical Assistance at the Crossroads

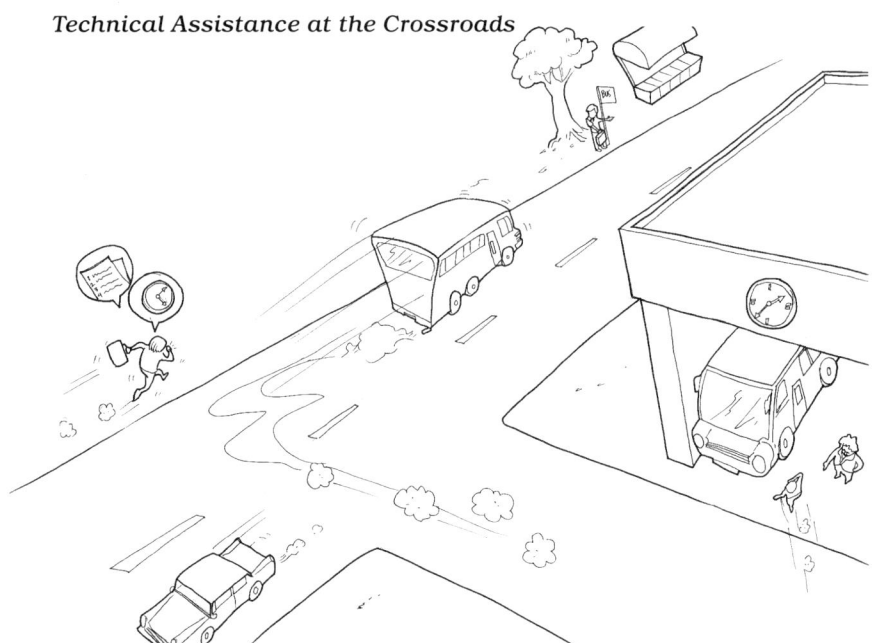

Managing Technical Assistance is not an easy task; it is about understanding a country partner's needs and delivering quality services by consultants. It is about learning from consultancy activities to be able to respond optimally to future needs. In fact, the Technical Support Facilities should provide an enabling environment for all stakeholders involved and build their capacity in addressing the HIV epidemic. TSF-WCA is now completing its first phase of activities; in assessing its performance, this is an ideal moment to evaluate the successes, the lessons learned, and the limitations. While envisioning a second phase, TSF feels it is at the crossroads in Technical Assistance management and has to make important choices.

---

[37] Yvonne Tavi Ouattara, Technical Support Facility for West and Central Africa (TSF WCA) Psycho sociologist, Capacity Building Adviser for French-speaking countries and Technical Support Manager for Civil Society.

Responding to AIDS in West and Central Africa

The West and Central African region is a multilingual environment with many countries in conflict or in post-conflict situations. The region has been severely affected by HIV epidemics. However, the funding which has increasingly been made available by national and international institutions to address these HIV epidemics has not always yielded the expected results. An obvious reason for this lack of success has been the unavailability of sufficiently skilled human resources. It was therefore considered necessary to build capacity to address the poor planning, monitoring, evaluation and management of the HIV responses in many countries in the region.

The Technical Support Facilities have been put in place by UNAIDS with the purpose of building local and regional capacity to effectively respond to HIV epidemics. TSF has addressed a number of capacity problems in WCA, such as the limited capacity within government and civil society to implement AIDS programs, insufficient capacities to deliver technical assistance, and lack of access to timely and high-quality short term technical support.

Assess the situation to provide Timely Quality Short term Technical Support

After the establishment of TSF WCA TA management they focused on
- Firstly, obtaining a better understanding of the region and country needs
- Secondly, establishing a core group of consultants with consultancy and technical skills to deliver good quality technical assistance.
- Thirdly, presenting its activities during inception visits to countries

Demand for services

These visits led to more TA requests and assignments. However, TSF WCA soon realized that it was not always clear what the request was really about and that it was important for the TSF to understand the situation in the region and for the country partners to express their needs clearly in the terms of reference for the assignment.

Knowledge of the work of partners

A good number of country partners working on HIV have shown a commitment in their national response, and developed HIV national strategic frameworks and operational plans. They are making an ef-

TSF WCA started its work in 2006 focusing on 12 priority countries. Due to time and resource limitations, it was impossible to cover all 25 TSF countries in the West and Central Region. The following criteria were used for the identification of those 12 priority countries:
- countries with a high HIV prevalence rate;
- countries with a high potential for work;
- countries in conflict or in a post–conflict situation;
- linguistic balance; and
- geographic spread.

In 2008 TSF has been able to scale up and is now covering all 25 countries in the region. However, some countries have more requests than others. This is also because the TSF is not equally well known everywhere. The inception missions are instrumental in introducing the TSF and its work to these countries and in building trust that the TSF can respond to their needs.
Backstopping has been provided to the TSF by a consultant who discussed marketing opportunities with TSF WCA.

---

fort to implement the Three Ones" principle of having one coordinating body, one strategic plan, and one monitoring and evaluation system. However, when TSF WCA analyzed the requests for technical assistance from these country partners, it was found that in practice, the link between these requests and the Three Ones principle was weak.

Analysis of the technical assistance requests revealed the following:
- Country partners did not have a system for technical assistance planning;
- Many requests had a short, sometimes unrealistic, timeframe between the TA request and the expected commencement;
- Some requests had unclear Terms of References;
- Only limited support by clients to the consultant(s) working on the assignment was envisioned;
- Consultants were sometimes not provided with documents and information ahead of time to enable sound preparation;
- The financial support was not always adequate;
- Clients were not always providing feedback on the TA provided.

Quality of technical assistance required
To respond to country partner's needs, consultants need to have

certain skills and competencies. Firstly, consultants need to have the ability to assess TORs and assess their own suitability and technical expertise for the assignment. This requires mature self-awareness and objective reasoning as to what they can and cannot accomplish. If in doubt, consultants should take the initiative and ask for clarification. Secondly, consultants need to prepare for their assignment and be proactive in sourcing documents and information. Thirdly, a consultant should be able to work in unfamiliar environments, with new people in multi-cultural settings, be open-minded, and be able to work independently. Last but not least, a consultant should be a good team-player and have excellent communication, writing, facilitation and effective self-management skills.

What action should TSF WCA take?
In order to ensure that consultants selected do meet with all the requirements outlined above, TSF WCA has introduced an enhanced quality assurance process and developed quality assurance guidelines that are shared with all partners. Furthermore, TSF WCA has organized a number of capacity development trainings for consultants. In total, twelve workshops have been organized, ranging from training in basic consultancy skills to technical skills such as monitoring, costing and budgeting. Also, 12 twinning assignments, whereby a senior expert is linked up with a junior consultant, have been organized.

TSF currently has about 500 regional consultants in its database. While this number is impressive, an analysis showed the following:
- Some consultants have poor self-awareness and overvalue their skills;
- Some consultants under-prepare assignments and do not proactively request information when needed;
- Certain technical skills are scarce in the database or region;
- Some consultants have demonstrated poor professional conduct (e.g. accepting work and then changing their mind after having signed the contract);
- Some consultants are not well-equipped to carry out work and expect others to provide support; and
- Some demonstrate poor writing skills and do not know how to structure reports. Collectively, these impediments are detrimental to the TSF-WCA's work and reputation, and if not checked, may be destructive.

Loyalty of consultants to TSF
Apart from the foregoing there are also other factors that influence the availability of good quality consultants. One is fierce competition for experienced consultants in the region. As TSF WCA is not the only agency trying to recruit the services of these consultants, winning the loyalty of these consultants who are very much in demand is a major challenge. One remedy deployed by TSF WCA is the offer of participation in the TSF capacity development training program for consultants free of charge. This is highly valued and appreciated by consultants, as they usually have to pay for professional trainings. Another strategy is the "the consultant's corner" in the TSF newsletter, through which consultants can share their view on the training and other services provided by the TSF. The best way to ensure loyalty is through ensuring that there are enough assignments to offer a number of key consultants regular work, and TSF WCA has entered into draw-down contracts[38] for this purpose.

Matching Demands and Services: What was done?
The TSF-WCA provided 3,882 TA days for the 25 countries (an average of six assignments per country) in the region, mainly in planning, monitoring and evaluation. Short term technical assistance has proven successful for countries because of the rapid turnaround in response to requests.

Upon receipt of a country partner's request, TSF screens the curriculum vitae (CV) of consultants listed in the database and selects the best three for a specific assignment from which the country partner can choose. However, a good CV is not enough of a premise on which to base this choice; consultants should be known to the TSF, so that accurate matching and a strong recommendation can be ensured. Photographs of the consultants are included in CVs for easy identification. The TSF technical support manager negotiates with the country partner and when needed assists the client with making a rational choice. This requires that the core group of consultants with whom TSF works are well-known to the TSF.

Another issue is the interaction between the consultant and the client. Sometimes a strong CV is chosen but the assignment still fails.

---

[38] The contract ensures a number of consultancy days for a small group of consultants by the TSF.

What has become apparent over time is the importance of an in-depth discussion on the TOR between the TSF, the consultant and the client at the outset of the assignment in order to become acquainted with one another, but more importantly to ensure that the assignment is well understood and that the prospective consultant is an appropriate candidate for the assignment.

Figures and statistics are usually the easiest way to demonstrate that programs work, but the quality of consultants can best be measured by gathering qualitative data regarding the satisfaction of the recipients. To measure this requires more than issuing a quality assurance form; it entails contacting the country partner directly to discuss their level of satisfaction and their feedback on the quality of the service provided.

The question is, however, how to link this feedback to the quality of the work done, which requires analyzing what is expressed by the client. Some qualitative tools could be developed to assist with this.

Establishing a system of providing quality technical support services

1 Data collection for Monitoring and Evaluation

Different tools are used by TSF to capture information on needs and satisfaction. During inception missions, TSF discussed country needs by meeting with key stakeholders (National AIDS Council, Ministry of Health, and Non-Governmental Organizations) and sharing findings in the form of a report with country partners. The inception exercise confirmed the earlier analysis of UNAIDS that led to the establishment of the TSFs, namely that of weak implementation capacity. UNAIDS Country Coordinators in general

> **Terms of Reference Model**
>
> **Key questions to be answered**
> - Why is the mission necessary?
> - What are the outcomes or deliverables?
> - Who will be involved and with what resources?
> - What is the budget?
> - When and where will the consultancy happen?
> - What type of consultant is needed for which tasks?
> - How will the consultancy achieve the objectives?

have sound insight about the needs of countries and can provide valuable advice on these needs as well as on the quality of the consultancy service provided.

> **ToR outline**
> - Background
> - Purpose and objectives
> - Scope and tasks
> - Services and outputs
> - Structure and composition of team
> - Specification skills
> - Deadline and timeframe
> - Reporting and accountability

Interaction on the TOR is challenging as the TSFs are remote from the field. However, by emphasizing the clarity of the TOR, the relation between capacity building and technical assistance can be strengthened. Some organizations have received special support for the development of TORs and TSF developed a TOR model which has been included in the consultation guide for country partners.

2 Discussion of ToR with partners

The TSF team first discusses the TOR with partners, and then with the consultant. In the final run, the three stakeholders have a joint discussion on the implementation of the assignment.
So far, these discussions on the TOR have not been recorded methodically in the TSF monitoring and evaluation system and this should be addressed. However, after having been in existence for three years, TSF WCA now discusses almost all TORs in detail with all parties involved.

3 Discussion of ToR with consultants

During the briefing of a consultant, the TSF looks into the consultant's understanding of the TOR and his or her skills. At the end of the assignment, the client is asked to complete an evaluation form. This is followed by a phone-call to the client during which the qualitative information provided in the form is verified. These calls are crucial because they allow the clients to clarify their feedback and provide additional and often very valuable information.

Lessons and Recommendations for continuity of quality technical support

The period of implementation yielded several lessons. Firstly, the availability of financial resources over time enabled better interaction with the actors on the ground. A slight restructuring and reorganization of TSF-WCA promoted more independent, better coordinated and stronger actions in the field. The loyalty policy ensured the availability of sought-after consultants, and the implementation of innovative, integrated capacity building activities enhanced the quality of technical assistance. Countries' responses are improved by the delivery of a comprehensive program that has integrated TA and capacity development. The quality assurance protocol has further strengthened the quality of the TA provided.

Other important learning points for country partners, consultants and TSFs are:

The participatory identification of needs may be time–consuming, but it is very beneficial for the person providing technical assistance. It is also the best way to ensure success and understanding among the counterparts. This process must include every stakeholder, especially those in vulnerable groups. The process will ensure a relevant TOR and a consultant who is best placed to respond to the specifications set out to meet the country partners' needs. The process also helps countries to identify persons who can provide follow up on the consultants' recommendations and ensures thorough reflection and mutual understanding of the TOR and better interaction between stakeholders and TSF. For consultants it is beneficial to work with a national counterpart, as this provides clarity on the context in which they work which broadens their knowledge base.

The TSF should promote more systematic transfer of skills during assignments. This could be done through ensuring integration of a capacity development element in the TOR. TSFs also have to ensure that the TOR is well understood and that the assignment is followed through and reinforced on the ground. Most importantly, TSFs should also promote that more resources should be allocated for enhancing consultants' skills.

3.3 Mission Impossible – Delivering Quality Output in a Short Time - Erastus Njeru[39] and Boaz Cheluget[40]

This case study has no connection to the work of the TSFs as such, but it is envisioned that through improved planning of technical assistance at country level with support of TSFs, situations described in this case study can be avoided.

Keeping Deadlines

One of the most important aspects of a successful consultancy assignment is the ability to meet the deadline, especially if the deadline is set internationally, hence it cannot be negotiated. This case study documents an assignment for which one month was allocated to carry out all the required tasks, whereas in the opinion of the consultant, the assignment should have been given at least two months, with the same resources.

The situation was exacerbated when one week of the allocated month was taken up with processing the funds, leaving only three weeks to carry out the activities.

By this time, there were many doubts as to whether it was possible to meet the deadline; –both the clients and the consultants thought that this was an impossible mission. All wondered what techniques the consultant could devise to achieve this deadline. *"This is suicidal,"* someone commented. Tempers flared at one point before the work commenced, with the consultant being unconvinced that the client could see the challenge posed by the unrealistic timeframe, while the client suggested that the consultant was fretting unduly and insisting that all the procedures should be fulfilled.

Developing Strategies to Cope with Time Constraints

The timeframe stipulated in the contract to conduct six national level HIV surveys was one month. Despite this constraint, the consultant devised strategies and cultivated an environment conducive to the completion of the assignment within the time allocated. The strategies which were conceived over the course of the assignment included:

---

[39] Erastus K. Njeru, B.Sc., M.Sc., HIV&AIDS M&E Consultant, University of Nairobi
[40] Boaz K. Cheluget, B.Sc., M.Sc., M&E Advisor, UNAIDS

- Use of a structured and cohesive data collection and supervision team
- Use of a large number of research assistants
- Use of mobile phones for follow-up and resolution of issues arising from field work
- Use of previously pre-tested questions for data collection
- Careful analysis and classification of the data requirements so as to optimize the movement of research assistants
- Having a large data entry team of 21 clerks working in three shifts of six or seven hours each

The environment which enhanced the success of the assignment included:

- An expectation of more assignments to follow
- A feeling of 'patriotism' and the satisfaction of contributing to the fight against AIDS
- Mutual respect amongst the team members

Terms for Consultant Services

An agreement was signed between the client and the consultant, requiring the consultant to carry out and report on six national level surveys on HIV related disease issues.

In the terms of reference written by the client, including the type of information and the populations defined, it was indicated that the client required results in six main areas, each with a different type of population definition and hence necessitating different sampling methods. Areas to be covered included the following topics:

HIV Policy environment – required interviews with the heads of Government departments, UN agencies and civil society organizations on their involvement in, commitment to and support for the creation of a conducive policy environment for an effective response to HIV;

- HIV policies and programs in the workplace – required visits to a selected number of organizations to investigate whether they had formulated/adopted policies and/or implemented various standard programs for AIDS;
- Life skills-based HIV education in schools – required visits to selected schools to investigate whether they had started providing life skills-based HIV education;

- Issues around support for orphans and their school attendance – required investigations on identified orphans and vulnerable children in selected households relative to the types of support their households were receiving, and whether the orphans were attending school; and,
- Youth issues related to AIDS – required to identify youth in selected households and assess their knowledge, attitudes on HIV issues and their associated practices.

The results were intended for use in international reporting; hence the surveys had to be carried out with sound methodological and statistical basis. Thus, the challenge was to assure high-quality, nationally representative and statistically sound results within a constrained timeframe.

Achieving the Miracle
It was clear from the beginning that accomplishing this task would require self-sacrifice, tact, tremendous effort, and some form of miracle so as to maintain integrity as a consultant. To achieve this, a systematic approach was necessary whereby decisions had to be

made with little room for error. The first important decision to be made was on the type of research team that could be used to complete the work. The composition of the team had to be informed by the data requirements.

The consultant executed careful analysis of the terms of reference. All the types of data required were listed and classified to determine which of them could be collected by the same individuals, so as to minimize movement of data collectors. This analysis revealed that the assignment could be subdivided into two segments, one requiring standard qualitative methods and the other requiring quantitative methods. This approach also guided the construction of the team.

Building a cohesive supervisory team was one of the other very important aspects of the organization of the assignment. Proper supervision by individuals other than the Team Leader would ensure that quality work would be produced simultaneously. The first decision was therefore to recruit two principal assistants who were assigned as senior consultants. Each of them took charge of one arm of the study. From then on, decisions on each arm of the study were made in consultation with the principal assistant/senior consultant. This decision enabled the simultaneous execution of the two arms of the assignment with most of the technical leadership being undertaken by the senior consultants.

Deliberations with the senior consultant for the qualitative arm indicated that there was a need to recruit one junior consultant. This incumbent would conduct key informant interviews and supervise several research assistants to collect data from the selected organizations using a pre-designed form.

The main challenge of completing the assignment on deadline was related to the technical team. Based on the time available, it was clear that there would only be between five and seven data collection days. Given that and the amount of data required, it was calculated that 40 research assistants were required. The decision was made to recruit eight supervisors, each responsible for eight research assistants. Each of the supervisors was given one geographical region to cover. Finally, a ninth supervisor was recruited to head the data entry team of 21 data entry clerks. Eventually, the following organogram evolved:

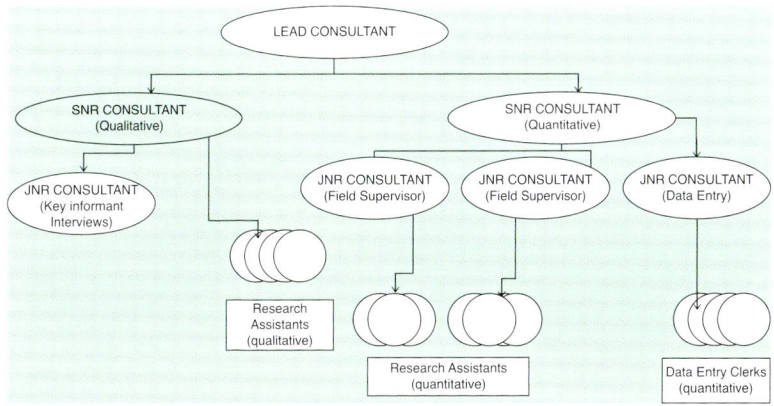

It was very important for the supervisory structure described above to function cohesively. One of the major considerations made in recruiting personnel was that each person had worked with the Team Leader on other projects previously, and they understood the importance of completing the work in time while maintaining quality. An important motivating factor was the learning opportunity that success in this assignment provided.

As far as possible, standard questionnaires and interview protocols to be used were taken as a whole or adapted from previously pre-tested instruments from reputable organizations such as UNAIDS or Family Health International (FHI). For the adapted instruments, approval in writing was obtained from the client.

For the results of the assignment to be acceptable to the client, proper methodology applicable to each data type had to be used to identify which of the study units were to be included in the sample. The sampling techniques used were convenience sampling for the qualitative part of the study, and multi stage random sampling for the quantitative data.
Field work processes were used for the qualitative methods of sub-studies. Individuals and organizations selected for the qualitative study did not present any special challenges as few of them were located outside the main city. These were all visited within one week.

However, the process of collecting data from all the corners of the country for the quantitative sub-studies presented a more serious challenge:

(a) Each group of research assistants (from each region) had to leave the city with all the forms that they required for the whole study. In the short time available, it was not possible to organize institutional transport for use by the research assistants.
(b) Research assistants were requested to use any means available to get to the selected households and schools.

The mobile phone was one of the most important tools for logistical arrangements, follow-up and resolving issues arising out of the field activities. On a routine basis, any research assistant who was not physically working alongside his or her supervisor had to call in to the supervisor at the beginning and at the end of each day, as well as at any time that they were moving from an area into another. The regional supervisors then briefed their supervising consultant at the end of each day on the coverage and any issues arising for onward transmission to the Team Leader. Through these calls, the supervisor was able to collect the completed questionnaires for checking and forwarding to the data entry centre.

Data entry started on the third day after the commencement of data collection – this required all supervisors to bring in their completed questionnaires for the first two days on the third day. To eliminate loss of data, each supervisor brought in batches of data recorded on a form tracking log.

Standard quality control activities were carried out in all the processes of the sub-studies. A one-day training of the research assistants was carried out, and pre-testing was done amongst them, as the items on the tools had been taken from standardized tools. Further, the items in the questionnaires were kept to a bare minimum (without compromising style and standard advice on questions).

At all times, the team leader was in charge of the quality of data collected; however, observing the chain of command was always encouraged. At the field level, regional supervisors conducted random visits to households to confirm information with household members.

Making the Impossible Possible
About 20 key informant interviews on policy environment were carried out as planned. In addition, two consensus-building workshops with stakeholders were held, during which findings for the Policy

Environment survey were presented. Consensus was achieved in the second meeting, and based on this, a narrative report containing the main findings was approved. For the workplace survey, 104 organizations were visited and key informant interviews carried out using a prescribed form.

A total of 2,101 households were visited and interviewed. From these households, 1,451 questionnaires on orphans and vulnerable children and 1,673 questionnaires on youth were completed. In addition, a total of 414 schools were visited and interviews were carried out with the school head or the deputy head. All these questionnaires were entered into SPSS, cleaned and analyzed. Final analyses of quantitative data were performed together with the client, and there were no complaints on quality.

All these activities were completed within the time stipulated in the contract. However, it was not without financial costs, nor without emotional and physical cost to the lead consultant. It should be noted that the lead consultant had less and less time to sleep as the activities progressed.

Analyzing the Impossible Task
This case study is probably an isolated instance and such situations would not be encouraged on a routine basis. While there may have been compelling reasons to have this assignment completed in haste, it should be noted that there is a high risk of burn-out, especially for the lead consultant, before the completion of activities. If this had transpired in this case, either the deadline would have been missed or the quality of the outputs would have been highly compromised.

One positive factor is that the client and the consultant had a cordial relationship prior to this assignment. Once the activities started, this helped to create an atmosphere conducive for closer collaboration and monitoring of progress by the client. In such a tight schedule, it is even more important for the consultant to give the client constant updates on progress and to have the client approve all the tools and the methodology to be used.

Recommendations out of the Mission Impossible Experience
Whereas it is important that adequate time be given to carry out assignments, high quality results may still be achieved through selfless dedication and innovative methods in logistical arrangements for an assignment.

- It is important that the client be very clear in their terms of reference, and understands the limitations of what can be achieved in a short time. Close collaboration between the client and the consultant in terms of elaborating the requirements is also an important factor for success in a consultancy.
- For consultants, it is advisable to familiarize themselves in all the methods and techniques that are currently in use within the consulting field even though they may be experts in one primary area.

Finally, even though the strategies and working environment described in this situation may have arisen out of the need to accomplish the tasks within the given time constraints, much of it should be applied even in ordinary circumstances to enhance the success of a consultancy.

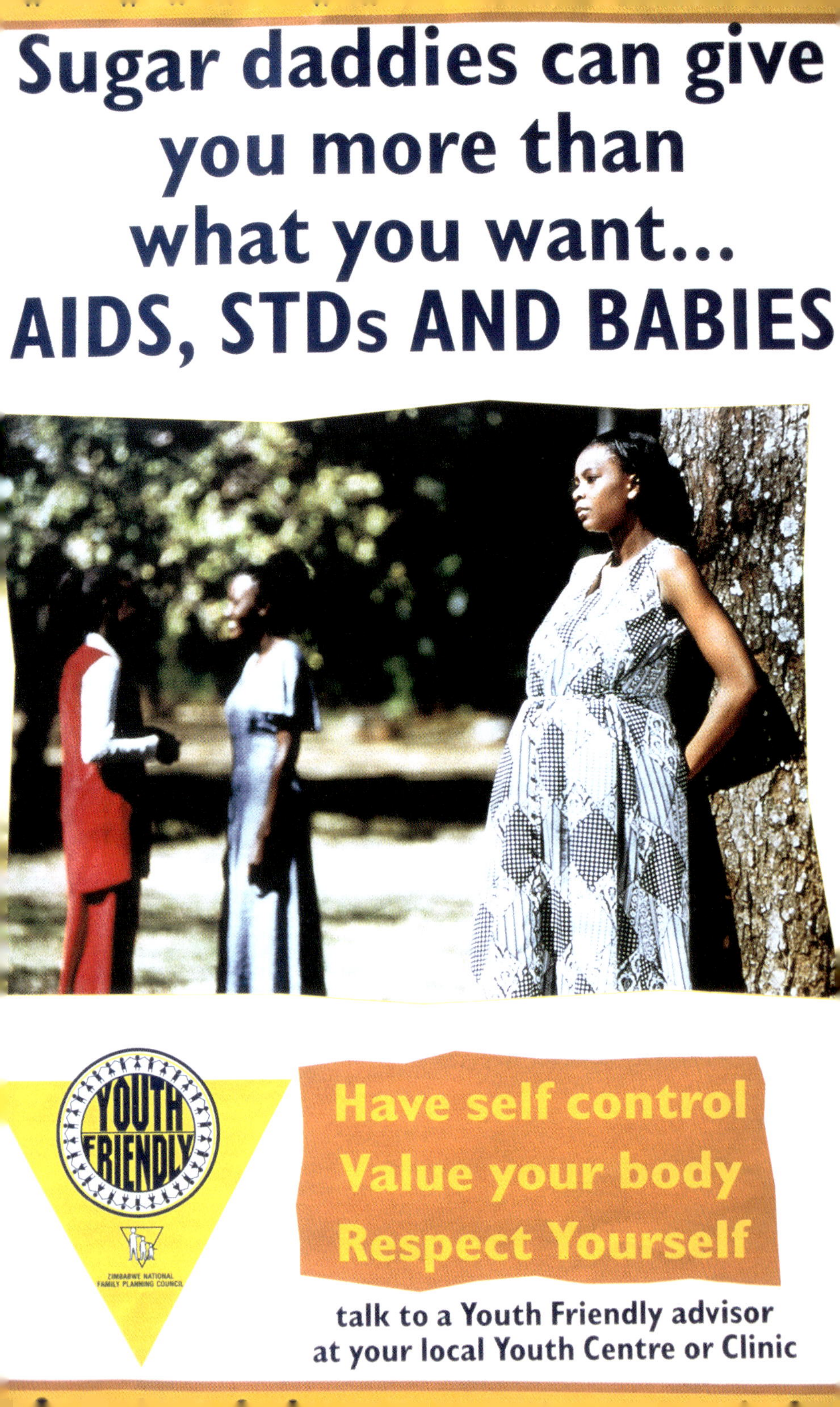

Sugar daddies can give you more than what you want...
AIDS, STDs AND BABIES

**Have self control
Value your body
Respect Yourself**

talk to a Youth Friendly advisor
at your local Youth Centre or Clinic

Chapter 4:
Cross-cutting lessons from the case studies

Tracing the diverse landscape of technical assistance (TA) and capacity development (CD) for the design, programming and implementation of effective national AIDS responses, the case studies in this book reflect the complex topography of the pandemic in its local, regional and global dimensions.

The case studies highlight that strong multi-sectoral leadership, governing well-trained personnel who execute soundly devised and properly costed strategies, will manifest successful national AIDS responses. The reality is nothing so simple. Just as the virus causes biomedical impairment in individuals and groups, shredding the social, economic and cultural fabric of nations, its effects also debilitate and damage country systems, deepening bureaucratic lethargy and in turn, the suffering of millions. In addressing the capacity crisis, as Stephen Lewis noted in 2006, the key to recovery – indeed, the key to subduing the entire pandemic – lies at country level.[41]

In some of the case studies, national partners' preparedness to HIV challenges is being viewed through the lens of country-specific realities. These case studies also show that where commonalities exist, regional collaboration fortifies solutions. In presenting findings from a wide range of settings and applications, the authors argue forcefully that this process needs to be evidence-informed and formulated around the needs articulated by the national partners.

To ensure leveraging and growth of information and learning around these endeavours, forging strategic alliances with other providers of technical support is a route that TSFs should consider with deliberate speed. Developing the capacity of consultants in the business practice areas that underpin AIDS response policy is imperative for

---

[41] United Nations. *Remarks by Stephen Lewis, UN Special Envoy for HIV AND AIDS in Africa, to the closing session of the XVI International AIDS Conference.* Toronto, August 18, 2006. www.un.org

reinforcing operational frameworks. Coordination of guidance and resources to bolster the proven strengths of TSFs as technical support providers is a key consideration for UNAIDS and other partners.

This book represents an invaluable body of practices and experiences yielding thematic and possible ways forward for different stakeholders:

For UNAIDS and partners

To ensure coordination and communication between UNAIDS and co-sponsors, and between UNAIDS and the TSFs, advocacy is needed for mobilization of resources to scale up capacity development activities. Efforts must be directed at promoting the ongoing integration of TA and CD components, as both areas of activity inform and complement one another. Harmonization of capacity development initiatives being undertaken by other partners should be supported. The introduction of process monitoring approaches for TA and CD activities will foreground key processes in the TSF model and the responsibilities of various stakeholders at critical nodes of practice. Standardizing good practices across TSFs can be achieved by producing and distributing a TA Policy and Process Manual. The M&E systems for TA and CD activities must be optimized to ensure that there are measurable outcomes. An unequivocal shift to evidence-informed and results-based planning processes is essential for maximum benefit to be rendered through national AIDS responses.

For the TSFs

The TSFs need to beneficiate the promising models assembled during their past years of implementation. They must build a knowledge management repository for case evidence which also sets up opportunities for information transfer and exchange between consultants and country partners. Reviewing lessons and experiences across the TA life-cycle and the global network of TSFs, collective energy should be directed towards faltering country systems. Using a participatory and inclusive approach, the work of strengthening quality assurance through integrated TA and CD must continue.

To establish and sustain an evidence informed and results-based context for action, the TSFs can and should generate more regional data on the pandemic to improve and update assessments of TA needs, and pursue collaboration with UNAIDS in providing capacity development for Results-Based Management (RBM) approaches. To maintain relevance and self-sufficiency, the TSFs own strategic planning around funding resources must be envisioned alongside and beyond the Technical Assistance Fund, towards diversification of funding resources.

CD of consultants

The TSFs need to invest vigorously in their consultant database membership, ensuring at the outset that orientation for consultants in the context of operational politics, culture, guidelines and Terms of Reference issues is conducted prior to them providing TA to clients and partners. Whilst consultants should be proactive in self-development using all available resources (including those of the TSF), the TSFs can augment the skills of consultants through a continuing experiential learning process, facilitating opportunities for the transfer of knowledge, and maintaining a vibrant suite of communication and marketing tools. Of particular importance is the production of evidence on the TSF experience in mentoring, twinning and coaching, and advocating for more funds for these activities.

CD of partners

Terms of Reference should reflect CD interventions that are carefully strategized to cultivate an inclusive ethos, to focus on addressing expressed country partner needs, to base planning on evidence using Results Based Management methodologies, and to reinforce the Three Ones principles[42]. CD of country partners should also prioritize developing long-term country capacity and establishing durable, authentic relationships with country partners. This process should include providing space for exchange of emerging data between implementers of National Strategic Plans, NACs, CCMs and other national partners for cohesive national efforts, in line with the Three Ones principles. In addition, with the rapid escalations in Global Fund grant funding, Grant Implementation support mechanisms and processes must be fostered. As HIV programs are implemented within national health systems – and many of these are buckling – strengthening of health systems remains a pivotal component of any national capacity development initiative.

---

[42] "Three Ones"; one national AIDS authority, one national strategic framework, and one national monitoring and evaluation system. UNAIDS. *2008 Report on the Global AIDS Epidemic*, Chapter 7, p.206. www.un.org

Finally, these case studies provide evidence that the provision of short-term technical assistance and capacity building through the UNAIDS model of Technical Support Facilities (TSF) has had a catalytic effect on the development of knowledge and processes for the effective implementation of national AIDS programs. Through multiple perspectives gleaned from lived experience on several continents, the case studies demonstrate that the TSF model is an essential package of technical support services for contributing to scaling-up HIV disease response. Building on the foundation of the past four years, regular sharing of ideas, practical experiences and reliable information between TSFs, and between TSFs and other TA providers, should be actively pursued.